"Boy, do I wish my kids (and I) had had this book when they were in school and college. Fortunately, my grandkids now will, and so will a pair of 'first generation' students whom my wife and I are trying to help get an education. We've found that knowledgeable, practical guidance is vital to their success. Thank you, Gordon, for supplying it!"

> —**Chester E. Finn, Jr., senior fellow at the**
> **Hoover Institution, Stanford University and**
> **president of the Thomas B. Fordham Institute**

"Gordon Green has written a book that every student and parent should read. Dispensing both common sense alongside expert insight, he offers invaluable guidance on everything from study tips to summer jobs. And all of it shared in jargon-free, readable prose chock-full of telling anecdotes. When I think back to my own trials with schools and studying, I only wish he had written this book a long time ago!"

> —**Frederick M. Hess, Ph.D., director of**
> **Education Policy Studies at the**
> **American Enterprise Institute**

"If every student and family read this book, our national dropout problem would disappear. It tells us why education is important, and, more importantly, how to succeed within the system, no matter your starting point."

> —**Indya Kincannon, chairperson of the Knox County**
> **Board of Education, Knoxville, Tennessee**

"As Dr. Gordon Green guides the student on a productive journey of acquiring new knowledge while making good grades with good job prospects, he involves the parents in the process, making learning a family affair. I highly recommend this book."

> —**Yung-Ping Chen, Ph.D., professor emeritus (Frank J.**
> **Manning Eminent Scholar's Chair in Gerontology,**
> **1988–2009) at the University of Massachusetts Boston**

"This important book is a grabber. Be grabbed and have a good life!"
>—**William P. Butz, president and CEO of**
>**Population Reference Bureau**

"Over the many years I have known Gordon Green, I have seen him dedicate himself selflessly to helping young Americans of every race, creed, color, and class. This has been of enormous service to the country he loves—and because Americans come from everywhere—it helps the world."
>—**Ben Wattenberg, host of PBS's *Think Tank* and**
>**senior fellow at the American Enterprise Institute**
>**and Hudson Institute, Washington, D.C.**

"Gordon Green's *Making Your Education Work for You* should be required reading for parents and students alike. Not only does he make the case for why education is so vitally important, he also provides a clear and accessible step-by-step guide to effective studying and classroom performance. His handbook for learning is a joy to read, a call to arms, and an inspiration."
>—**Kathleen D. McCarthy, Ph.D., professor of history and**
>**director of the Center on Philanthropy and Civil Society,**
>**the Graduate Center, City University of New York**

"There are no gimmicks here, just good, solid advice about how to work hard, how to work efficiently, and how to train your memory to the important stuff. Green focuses on the crucial insights a student needs to grasp day by day, chapter by chapter, semester by semester."
>—**Michael Novak, George Frederick Jewett Scholar**
>**in Religion, Philosophy, and Public Policy at the**
>**American Enterprise Institute, Washington, D.C.,**
>**former U.S. ambassador, and recipient of the**
>**Templeton Prize for Progress in Religion**

"*Making Your Education Work for You* can help students achieve what many may think is impossible: straight A's in every class, semester after semester. . . . Now, with the help of Dr. Green's easy-to-follow system, I can help my students and my child succeed in school and in life. Thank you, Dr. Green!"

"This is an excellent guide, in clear common-sense language that will help all students improve their study and performance—even very good students."

"In his book, Gordon Green describes the crucial link between education and obtaining satisfying and economically rewarding work. Even more important for readers, however, is the encouragement he provides to both youth and their parents by describing an approach that will enable them to take full advantage of their opportunities to learn and to succeed."

"The most inspiring college teacher I ever had opened his class with the Latin phrase: '*Tuum est*' (i.e., 'It is up to you.'). Green's book superbly prepares any aspiring student as to how to respond to this educational challenge."

"Alchemy is the power of transforming the ordinary into something valuable. Dr. Green is an education alchemist with a winning formula for success. Students who read this book will learn how to harness knowledge and make it work for them both in their careers and in the enjoyment of life. Not least, parents will learn how to help their children become self-confident and better understand the importance of education in achieving job and income goals."

—Alfred Tella, former research professor of
economics at Georgetown University

Student Praise

"*Making Your Education Work for You* is reader friendly to both high school and college students. I began using Dr. Green's study techniques in college when I was a struggling student and have earned A's ever since! Now, as a licensed school psychologist, I still utilize his ten-point study system to help struggling high school and college students."

—Jason Mathison, M.A., CAGS, NCSP, ABSNP,
Virginia Licensed School Psychologist
Diplomate, American Board of School Neuropsychology

"As a student, realization of your dreams begins with the courses you take in school and the grades you receive. I used Dr. Green's study methods to realize my dreams of becoming a successful dentist, finishing first in my class in dental school, earning a fellowship to the Mayo Clinic, and receiving the equivalent of hundreds of thousands of dollars in scholarships in the process. I enthusiastically recommend his new book to my own children and to my patients, and I encourage the same for you to make your dreams become a reality!"

—Dr. Robert Semco, D.M.D., M.S., Middletown, Rhode Island

"I was already a huge fan of Gordon Green's work. The study habits I learned from one of his earlier books enabled me to graduate summa cum laude from UCLA (quite a difference from the C's, D's, and E's I got in high school!). His new book, *Making Your Education Work for You,* shows parents how to demonstrate the importance of education to their children and shows students exactly what they need to do to be successful in school and life. Had the

information in this book been available to my parents when I was growing up, I can say without a doubt that my childhood and my relationship with my parents would have been much happier. If you have tried everything you can think of to motivate your child to work hard in school but with no success, GET THIS BOOK. It will change your life!"
—Joseph Denney, Esq.

"Over a decade ago, Dr. Gordon Green's earlier book *Getting Straight A's* was instrumental in transforming me from a poor student in high school into a straight-A 'overachiever' in college. This time Dr. Green has done it again with his new book, *Making Your Education Work for You*. Students both young and old will discover methods that help to accelerate learning, improve comprehension, make better grades, and give hope to those who have perpetually struggled in school. More than that, however, Dr. Green presents a powerful case for the importance of education in today's global economy and shows you how to improve your competitive position so you can realize the benefits."
—Bradley Chapple, owner of Aspen Computer Services, Fort Collins, Colorado

"Years ago, I sat alone on the Rutgers University campus with a 1.9 grade point average, a copy of Gordon Green's book *Getting Straight A's*, and little else. Now twenty-one years later I can look at my diploma, which states that I graduated with highest honors. After reading his latest book, *Making Your Education Work for You*, I'm excited to share his ideas with my students and to put his proven methods to work in my daily life. Simply stated, Gordon Green's writing changed my life. He's my long-distance, secret mentor."
—Michael S. Casella, teacher at East Amwell Township School, Ringoes, New Jersey, and featured columnist at BleacherReport.com

Also by Gordon W. Green, Jr., Ph.D.

Getting Straight A's

*How to Get Straight A's in School
and Have Fun at the Same Time*

Helping Your Child to Learn

Helping Your Child to Learn Math

Getting Ahead at Work

Making Your Education Work for You

A Proven System for
Success in School
and for Getting the
Job of Your Dreams

GORDON W. GREEN, JR., PH.D.

A Tom Doherty Associates Book · New York

A Forge Book
Published by Tom Doherty Associates, LLC
175 Fifth Avenue
New York, NY 10010

www.tor-forge.com

Forge® is a registered trademark of Tom Doherty Associates, LLC.

ISBN 978-0-7653-1952-4 (hardcover)
ISBN 978-0-7653-1953-1 (trade paperback)

First Edition: June 2010

Printed in the United States of America

0 9 8 7 6 5 4 3 2 1

Dedicated to the memory of
Catherine Disney Gregory
(1916–2006)

Contents

PART 1

For Parents and Students

The Importance of Education

PART 2
For Students
What You Will Have to Do

Acknowledgments

Any book is a lengthy endeavor that requires the efforts of several individuals. This one is no exception. Because this is a book about parents working with students, first and foremost I want to thank my own parents, Gordon and Marie Green, for all the time they spent emphasizing the importance of a good education to me when I was growing up. I was as hardheaded as anyone when I was a young man, and more so than most, but as I have gotten older, I have come to realize and appreciate all the good values they taught me over the years. I would also like to thank my three children, Heidi Riemenschneider, Dana Green, and Chris Green, for the fruitful interactions I had with them when they were in school, because their experiences certainly taught me much about how to write this book. In addition, I would like to thank my daughter Dana for her assistance in reviewing the manuscript. As always, my dear wife, Maureen Green, was very understanding as I shirked many of my usual household duties while engaged in this endeavor. I also want to thank my longtime friend and literary agent, the late Harold Roth, whose wise counsel and unwavering support over the years have made this effort and all my previous books possible. Last, but not least, I want to thank my publisher and editor, Kathleen Doherty, who always adds something significant to my work and makes me sound much better than I really am.

Starting the Journey

Parents and Students:

The secret of success is constancy to purpose.

—*Benjamin Disraeli,*
former British prime minister

Parents try to instill the importance of education in their children from the earliest years, but their efforts often fall on deaf ears. With additional experience, parents realize that the type and amount of education determine who gets the good jobs, not just in terms of pay but also in terms of duties and responsibilities. They also realize that a good education provides the resources needed to live the good life (however they choose to define it). If only children could understand at an early age what parents have come to know through long years of experience.

It is very difficult for parents to communicate the critical importance of education to children, particularly when youngsters do not have the responsibilities of parents, such as taking care of families and paying the bills. Parents (rightly) do not want their children to be concerned with these responsibilities when they are young, because they know that children need a happy, carefree childhood to evolve into a successful, well-adjusted adult. At the same time, parents also want their children to understand the importance of education at an early age so they can start building a lifelong foundation that will help them succeed in life. And this is where the rub comes in: Getting children to understand the importance of education before they have had the experience to appreciate it is one of the most difficult tasks imaginable.

If a child does not have the basic skills to succeed in school, or has had an unpleasant experience at school, the task of instilling the importance of education is made that much more difficult. It is a basic fact of human nature that we all like what we are good at, even from our earliest years. If a child has not been a successful student in the past, then he or she is likely to regard school with disdain. If parents value education—and I assume they do or they would not be reading this book—then they know that when a child is not living up to expectations it is one of the most stressful experiences imaginable. Each evening they will struggle with a student who does not really want to learn, is not willing to put in the time needed to succeed, and who will complain continually about going to school. A child might fall in with a peer group that embraces similar negative attitudes about school, which will make the task of communicating with him or her that much more difficult.

Because education involves adding more information to a well-established foundation, the further behind a student falls the more difficult the task becomes to catch up, and that is when problems arise. Stressful arguments over school occur regularly between parents and children at home, and parents often take the worry with them to work the next day. Face it: If a child is not succeeding at school, his or her parents' life will be miserable! And when parents make a last-ditch effort for their child to understand the importance of education, they find that he or she is more willing to listen to the members of his or her peer group than to them. The purpose of this book is to help parents and students avoid or overcome this unhappy state of affairs, which can be tantamount to a torture chamber if it has progressed too far.

I provide a general introduction on the importance of education that is intended for both parents and students to read. The book is then divided into two parts: the first for parents and students and the second primarily for students, although parents are certainly invited to read the second part as well. Knowing the details of what makes a good student helps parents to reinforce the principles continually to their children. The conclusion, titled "It's a Wrap," is intended for both parents and students.

In the first part, I present a number of arguments that illustrate the importance of education. First, I provide an overview of how a good education and good job translate into a good life, not just in meeting the basic needs of life but in developing the capacity to enjoy life more fully. Second, I relate a number of stories about the experiences of others who have had difficulty with their studies, including your author, before getting on the proper road for success. Third, I discuss the beauty of knowledge, to instill a love of learning that will help both parents and students enjoy the road that lies ahead. Fourth, I describe the value of making good grades, both in terms of building confidence and self-esteem, and in expanding opportunities. Finally, I present arguments on how a good education will lead to a good occupation, one that not only pays well financially but is also meaningful and enjoyable to practice.

In the second part, I provide students with a compact summary of the tools that they will need to succeed in school. First, I present the techniques necessary to master the basic skills, such as how to read a book to gain the greatest comprehension, how to take different types of tests to obtain the highest scores, and how to write a term paper that will be enjoyable to prepare and will make a genuine contribution. Second, I present my proven ten-point study system for making straight A's in school, covering all the essentials, such as how to plan a course of study, how to gain the maximum understanding of material presented in class and from reading assignments, and how to prepare for examinations to receive the highest marks. Third, I present a number of tips to show students when, where, what, and how to study so they can make my system work for them with the least effort and greatest payoff.

Learning may be a lifetime effort, but the foundation needed for future growth is built in the early years with a cooperative effort between parents and their students. That is why I have written a book addressed to both audiences, so they can work together to achieve success. The ancient Chinese philosopher Lao-tzu said, "A journey of a thousand miles must begin with a single step." Parents and students: You have taken that first step, now let's get on with the journey.

GORDON W. GREEN, JR.
Fairfax Station and
Charlottesville, Virginia

Introduction

French author François de La Rochefoucauld said, "We may give advice, but we do not inspire conduct." Parents may give advice to their children, but that does not necessarily mean that they will follow it.

I am sure that students have heard statements a thousand times or more from their parents, teachers, friends, and relatives about why they need to do well in school. I am now a grandfather, and my school days are long behind me, but I can still hear those statements in the back of my mind, almost as if they were said only yesterday. "You need to get good grades or you won't get into a good college . . . You need to go to a good college or you won't get a good job . . . You need to get a good job or you won't have enough money . . . If you don't have enough money, your life will be miserable." And so it went. My parents, teachers, friends, and relatives would tell me the same things a thousand times in a thousand different ways, but at the time the words meant nothing to me. They were like water rolling off a duck's back. The biggest problem was that no one explained to me what these words *really* meant, so I ignored them completely and went about doing other things that I enjoyed or thought were more important at the time.

As I look back now, and actually as I began to realize quite a long time ago, there is a lot of truth to those words—not absolute truth, but enough truth to make one stand up and listen. If you look carefully at those words, you will see a well-defined sequence of events. It is almost as if you have to get through one door before you can go through the next door, and if you fail to get through any one door then all of the following doors are closed to you. What I am really saying is that the United States economy and job market operate in a certain way, and like it or not, they *will* influence your future life and personal livelihood. And if you do not like the way "the system" operates, or you think it is unfair, don't think you are the one who is going to change things for the better. Many have tried and more have failed. The goal is to understand how the system operates so you can adjust your behavior to profit from it. That is why I have titled this book, *Making Your Education Work for You.*

Before we take a close look at how the system operates, there is one point that I want to make up front, and it is one of the most important things that I am going to tell you. As I have grown older, the one thing I have truly learned is that there is pure enjoyment in learning for its own sake. When I made this statement to my children they called me a nerd, a weirdo, or worse—and I told them that someday they would understand what I meant. I am not even talking about the enjoyment and pride students will receive from getting good grades in school, or not hearing parents and others yell at them anymore, although that will certainly come, too. What I am talking about is the sheer enjoyment from learning how and why things operate as they do.

Let's face it: It is a big, complicated world out there with so much advanced technology that no one can understand how everything really works. There is much mystery in the world, and we are forced to take a lot for granted just to function in it. But understand that there is a logic and a scientific explanation for just about everything that happens, whether it is how a child is born, why an airplane stays aloft, or why we are having such a difficult time fighting certain deadly diseases. If you can understand these and a variety of other things, each day of your life will be more meaningful and enjoyable.

Now let's take a closer look at how "the system" really operates. I might add that I get a lot of enjoyment from doing this sort of thing because I am an economist by training (Ph.D. in economics) and what economists basically do is figure out how and why the economy works the way it does. I ask for one ground rule up front: I will be very candid in telling you how things actually work if you will keep an open mind in listening to what I have to say. Don't make a judgment too quickly!

Let's start off with the first statement: "You need to get good grades or you won't get into a good college." The job of the college admissions officer is to make sure that the college attracts the strongest students possible for its entering freshman class. That is an important factor in how the school attains and retains a high ranking with *U.S. News and World Report* (which does the college rankings); keeps the professors happy who want knowledgeable, hard-working students in their classrooms; and keeps the alumni happy who make donations to the school to keep it financially sound. Every year brings a new competition with the best schools trying to get the best students, the second-best schools trying to get the second-best students if they cannot attract the best students, the third-best and lower-order schools settling for the students who are left, all the way down to students who were not able to get into the school of their choice or who need additional preparation and have decided to attend a junior or community college until their choices are more attractive.

How do the college admissions officers make a decision on the best students, a task complicated by the fact that they have never met the vast majority of the students who apply to their schools? The answer is that they have to rely on certain key indicators, such as the types of courses students took in high school, the grades they received in those courses, the scores they earned on standardized tests such as the SAT/ACT, or other factors such as their letters of recommendation, how well they did on their admissions essays, or the number of extracurricular activities in which they were involved. Face it— the admissions officers don't know the students who applied, so they need to rely on what they see on a piece of paper. The thinking is that students who took the right subjects such as Advanced Placement courses will have adequate preparation for college, and if they received good grades they understood the material and have good work habits that will serve them well in college.

But it does not stop there! The fact is that college admissions officers do not trust all high schools, because they know that some schools offer watered-down courses or are very generous in giving high grades. So they feel that they need to grade the high schools in some way, and that is why they look for a generalized indicator of how much students really know, such as their scores on standardized tests. Letters of recommendation contain useful information about what teachers actually think of students, which may be different than what is indicated by their grades, and how well they think students will do in college. Written essays give admissions officers a chance to see how students actually think, how well they can express themselves, and perhaps even an indication of their moral values. Extracurricular activities are always desirable, because no school wants only a bunch of drones who lock themselves in their dormitory rooms and contribute nothing to campus life.

Taking all of this information into account, admissions officers are able to rank aspiring students from the highest to the lowest and decide who they want to make offers to for admission. Of course, all of the colleges are going through a similar process, and odds are that they come up with similar lists of desirable students who applied to multiple schools. The best students will get their choice of which college to attend, and if they are really good—that is, if they *look* really good (no one knows how good they are until they actually perform)—they may get a scholarship or other financial support.

The point to emphasize is that of all the factors I have mentioned concerning what admissions officers look at, good grades are the most important. Why? Because good grades not only indicate what students are capable of doing but what they have actually done! Nothing speaks like a track record, because behavior often repeats itself. Students with high scores on standardized tests may be capable of doing a lot, but who knows if they will actually perform? As in all endeavors in life, execution is what counts. And if students do not have good grades in high school, they may not get through that first door that opens the way for them to get through the other doors during the rest of their lives.

Now let's look at the second statement: "You need to go to a good college or you won't get a good job." I am going to amend that statement slightly by adding that not only do you need to have gone to a good college, you also need to have earned good grades while you were there. Recognize that what we are talking about here are the jobs for which a college degree is required, not the multitude of jobs out there that do not require any college training. After receiving a bachelor's degree a student may decide to go directly into the job market, or go to graduate school for more specialized training (what I have to say applies to both). Like college admissions officers, employers looking at prospective employees also do not know them personally, so they need to rely initially on what is written on a piece of paper. Employers have one big advantage over college admissions officers, however, because if they like what they see on that piece of paper, they can invite the person in for a job interview to obtain more information and find out how he or she might fit into the office or work setting.

In many respects, employers face challenges very similar to those of college admissions officers. Because they do not actually know all of the characteristics about aspiring employees, they need to rely on certain signals. The courses students take in college are an important signal to employers because they indicate whether job applicants received the necessary background to do the work. While no courses taken in college will exactly provide the skills needed to do a job, what they really teach students is the ability to think, which can be used to learn what is required in a job. Perhaps the most important signal to employers is the grades students received in college. Good grades indicate an ability to learn difficult material and the willingness to stick with a curriculum to successful completion, the same skills that are required for success in a job setting. Moreover, good grades suggest that a person will be very trainable. Employers also grade the college, because they know that some are much tougher than others and do a better job of preparing students for the world of work. Employers put a very high premium on recommendations from professors, because they want to know what the job candidate is like as a person and whether he or she will fit comfortably into their job setting.

When a student is applying to graduate school, all of the factors I have mentioned are even more important. The best graduate schools will accept only students who have taken the courses required to master material at the next higher level, and who received very good grades in the process. Written essays indicate how well students can express themselves, and whether their interests are aligned with those of the graduate program. They will also want to know how well students did on standardized tests such as the Graduate Record Examination (GRE) because, again, they do not trust the preparation and grading of all colleges, and they want to know how much students know in an objective sense. Letters of recommendation from key professors are also very important, especially from those who are well recognized or highly respected, because graduate admission committees put much more value in an assessment from someone they know and trust than what is on a piece of paper. Forget about extracurricular activities at this level, because they do not really matter. If a student comes across as very capable, he or she may get a teaching fellowship or research assistantship, and actually be paid to go to graduate school!

By now, you should start to appreciate the importance of getting good grades all through school. Without them, one of those early doors will not open, and it will be more difficult to get through the rest!

The third statement was: "You need to get a good job or you won't have enough money." First of all, good jobs are, as they say, "in the eyes of the beholder." What is a good job to me or someone else may not be a good job to you. Some educated people love to do science and work in a laboratory, whereas other educated persons would view this as a form of mental torture. Some people like to work on difficult projects all by themselves, and others like to work in the company of others. Some would rather work indoors in a fixed setting, while others would rather work outdoors or travel. We should all be grateful that different people like different jobs, because if everyone wanted to do the same job there would not be enough of them to go around and the essential work of society

would not get done. The important point here, however, is
that if you are an educated person and have the necessary
skills, then you can *choose* the type of job that is desirable in
your own eyes. The less education you have the less choice
you will have, and at some point you may be forced to take a
job that is not to your liking, just to earn a living.

Now here is the most important point of all: The more desirable jobs tend to be the ones that pay the most money! If
you are doing a job that requires only manual labor and not
much skill, ability, or thought, then the pay will likely be low
because just about anyone can do it. You will also find such
jobs to be the most tiring physically and boring mentally. If
you have a college degree (or higher), then you had to spend a
lot of time, money, and effort getting that degree, not to speak
of the forgone earnings while you were going to school, and
the employer has to pay you more to do the job. Why are employers willing to do this? The answer is simple: With more
education and training you will be able to do the job at a
higher level and earn more money for the employer. Remember, at least in theory, no company is going to pay you more
than the amount of money you can earn for them, because to
do so they would be losing money. So, the interesting result is
that with more education you get to select the type of job that
you find desirable and earn more money for doing it.

Persons with a good education can expect their income
to increase over most of their working lives. Individuals with
college or higher degrees will find that their income continues to rise as they gain more experience in the working world.
They have a significant advantage over persons with less
education when competing for positions that require greater
skills or offer supervisory responsibilities. In contrast, persons without college degrees often find themselves in positions in which income flattens out even as more experience is
obtained. Because their education is limited, they may never

have the chance to get into a job that has a steeper earnings profile over time. As a result, the earnings differences between college-educated persons and those with less education often get magnified over time. As adults, the two groups end up with very different levels of income. It is not that people with lower levels of education do something wrong in their careers; many just never get a chance to show what they are capable of doing because they get locked into dead-end jobs. Education decisions affect lifetime income.

Finally, let's take a look at the fourth statement: "If you don't have enough money your life will be miserable." My grandfather used to say, "Money may not be the most important thing in the world, but it is way ahead of whatever is in second place." Truly, once you have enough money to live comfortably, you realize that there are many more important things such as freedom (I mean *true* freedom, to do whatever you want whenever you want to do it), peace of mind, or even pursuit of an activity that you consider desirable. If you do not have enough money to be comfortable, then your life really will be miserable, particularly if you are always scraping to make ends meet. Few things in life cause more stress and tension than a lack of money. For most people, the job they have is how they spend most of their time (even more than they spend with their families), becomes part of their identity, and is the major source of income that will determine how well they live. If you have a good job that pays plenty of money, your life will be more rewarding in many ways.

It is difficult for most young people to realize how important money is to their future success and happiness. Let's face it: When students are living at home, most of their expenses are taken care of by their parents. Students probably think of money when they need it for something specific to buy, such as clothing, a DVD, or an admission ticket to a concert. But think for a minute about what it costs today to buy a house, furniture to put into a house, cars, insurance, food, gasoline and other energy bills, and so forth, not to speak of the taxes that various levels of government will collect before you even get to spend your money. The biggest drain on your finances will be a house, and buying a first home is the biggest challenge of all. If you live in a major metropolitan area, the cost of a house of given quality varies tremendously with its location, because people will pay dearly to live in a desirable location. If you do not have enough money to buy the house, there is another door closed to you. By having a good job that pays a plentiful income, you can save money more rapidly to make the dream of owning a home become a reality.

Now I want you to think more broadly about what is likely to happen in the future. The United States is the world's most developed economy, with the highest levels of income, but there will be pressures on this in the future. Consider first the pressures at home. There is a group called the "baby boom" generation, the roughly seventy-eight million people who were born in the United States during the two decades (1946 to 1964) following World War II. Many of them are retiring and living longer, causing Social Security and Medicare expenditures to increase dramatically. Because birth rates have declined, there will be greater pressures on people in the younger generation to work longer or pay higher taxes to cover these expenses. Now consider the pressures abroad. Although the United States is still preeminent in the world in technological knowledge, other nations are beginning to catch up. The wage scales in these other countries are usually much lower, and many businesses have relocated their operations overseas to cut costs. Although many of these developments are desirable because each nation should produce what it does best, there are likely to be pressures on wages for people in the younger generation. Believe me, you are going to need the best job you can get and the highest income you can earn to maintain a high standard of living.

Now I want you to think very broadly, beyond your immediate interests. The United States is the world's only superpower, and our policies set the tone for much that happens in the world. The United States has played a major role in encouraging the spread of democracy and freedom throughout the world. Today there are major threats to our way of life, some of them in the form of terrorism and others in the form of certain nations that do not like the ideas of democracy and freedom because they will not be able to control their citizens. But the simple fact is that democracies are desirable because they do not wage war on each other and they maximize the welfare of their citizens. How do you think the United States got to be the world's only superpower? It is only because of the highly skilled and trained men and women in our workforce who get up every morning, go to work, and do their jobs to the best of their abilities. Our young persons will soon be among them, and if they are educated they will be able to perform their role at the highest level. It is essential that these young persons succeed, because there is nothing less at stake than our entire way of life.

Wow! I know that this is a lot to dump on students and parents, and there are probably many other things that you would rather be thinking about than your future problems or the problems of the world. But the things I have told you are true, and they will influence your life for the rest of your days. If young people realize these challenges at an early age, then they will understand the importance of doing their best in school, and apply themselves accordingly.

One of the true beauties of the United States is that each of us can become whatever he or she wants in life. We do not live in a caste system in which people are forced to follow the occupation of their father or mother, as some countries still practice. If you want to become a doctor or a lawyer, you can go to medical school or law school, pass your exams, and realize your dreams. You can pursue any other occupation you want, as long as you obtain the necessary education and training, and apply yourself. Moreover, we are a nation of second chances . . . and third chances . . . and fourth chances . . . or as many chances as you want! If you decide later that you want to go back to school and get the necessary education to enter another occupation, then you can do that. But recognize that it gets progressively harder as you get older. Older persons have the responsibilities of working to earn a living, or supporting a family, and it becomes more difficult for them to make career changes later on—but it can still be done!

Another thing needs to be stated up front about the different challenges each of us face. A young person from a wealthy family has several advantages. When a family has money, its children may not have to work during the school year or summer because the family will pay tuition bills at college and other expenses. Students have a big advantage in life if they do not need to take out education loans that will have to be repaid once they start working. A young person from a family without much money faces a much larger challenge. Getting enough money to go to college is always a challenge, and the student may have to work during the school term to obtain the money, which leaves less time available for study. It may take years of hard work to repay all of the education loans. Nevertheless, a college education is attainable even for students without much money if the desire is present. My family had a moderate income, and I was only the second person in my entire extended family to attend college; the first was my uncle, Andy Davis, Jr., who obtained an athletic scholarship to college, and went on to play professional football for the Washington Redskins. Students interested in learning more about the availability of student loans and financial aid will find suggested online links in the section titled "Educational Resources" (appendix C) at the back of this book.

Regardless of your personal situation, my goal is twofold: (1) To motivate parents and students about the importance of school, and (2) to provide the basic tools so they can be successful in working together to accomplish their objectives. The remainder of this book is devoted to the accomplishment of these two objectives.

In part 1 I provide a number of perspectives and arguments that parents can use to convince their students about the importance of education. In chapter 1, "How a Good Education and Good Job Translate into a Good Life," I highlight the significant demographic, social, and economic changes that have taken place in our society, and discuss how a good education is needed for a person to prosper in today's world. I then present some convincing statistics that will show students what to expect in the way of income from all of their efforts, and discuss how this will help them live the kind of life they desire.

A large part of believing in anything lies in knowing the experience of others. In chapter 2, "Others Who Have Had Difficulty in School Have Succeeded," I start off by telling you my story, because in terms of performance I have at times been one of the worst students imaginable and at others one of the best students imaginable. My grades in high school were so poor that I had to go through a remedial program to get into college, but in graduate school I made an A in every course, test, and paper to earn my Ph.D. (and that was while working at a full-time job). When I tell you my story, you will be able to see what was going through my mind when I was a poor student as well as when I was a good student, and you will realize that any student can do the same.

I then tell you some stories about the experiences of others—some who were very poor students; some who were average students; and some who already were good students, but wanted to become even better students. All of them had a set of things in common: They started to believe in themselves, began to enjoy school more, and raised their grades significantly, many becoming straight-A students. Some went on to the occupation of their dreams, such as becoming a medical doctor. When you hear their stories, you will know that what I am going to tell you applies to anyone regardless of age, race, sex, or other personal characteristics, and that it can also apply to you.

In the remaining chapters of part 1, I discuss a number of additional topics that will help the reader appreciate the value of a good education. Chapter 3, "The Beauty of Knowledge," examines how the attainment of knowledge enriches peoples' lives and understanding of the world, enabling them to obtain more enjoyment from everything they do. Chapter 4, "The Value of Getting Good Grades," is presented not only from the economic standpoint discussed earlier, but also emphasizes how students can obtain maximum enjoyment from the educational experience and build personal confidence and self-esteem. It is never too soon for students to start thinking about the type of occupation that they want to pursue. In chapter 5, "How to Engage in Effective Job Planning," I present a simple approach that will help students start thinking about the type of occupation and industry in which they want to be employed, so they will be motivated to take the right courses in school and score highly in them to make the dream become a reality.

In part 2, I present an organized system of study that shows students how to be successful in school. I have devoted much of my life to helping students succeed in my earlier books on *Getting Straight A's* (for college students) and *How to Get Straight A's in School and Have Fun at the Same Time* (for high school students and below). In the present book I bring all of this knowledge together to show students how to make top grades and enjoy the educational experience. The focus of the discussion is for high school students and students entering or already in college or graduate school.

Part 2 is organized into three chapters that include all of the skills needed to become a straight-A student. In chapter 6, "Mastering the Basic Skills," I start out with essential skills such as how to read books to gain maximum understanding from them, strategies for taking different types of tests to ensure a high score, and how to write a paper while enjoying the experience. In chapter 7, "A System for Getting Straight A's," I present my ten-point study system that shows students how to prepare adequately for class, understand the maximum amount of information presented by instructors, and prepare for examinations in a painless way. Finally, in chapter 8, "Making the System Work for You," I present a series of study tips on who, what, where, when, how, and why to study, so students can complete their schoolwork in an efficient manner and still have ample time for all of the other things that they want to do!

The conclusion, titled "It's a Wrap," brings together all of the ideas presented in the book, and develops a strategy that will help students develop persistence in obtaining long-range goals. Appendix A provides a suggested reading list for students who want to prepare for their next year of study. Appendix B provides a list of key words frequently used in examinations, and describes exactly what they call for in providing a good answer. Appendix C provides online links for several educational resources that are useful to readers. Appendix D contains my academic transcript, showing courses I took and grades I received while earning my Ph.D. in economics from George Washington University.

In summary, the strategies presented in this book provide a complete road map that shows parents and students how to work together for success in school. Parents will know the messages that are important to communicate to their students, and students will know what is needed for success. Mutual reinforcement is the winning combination that will make success a reality.

RECAP

This book provides a systematic approach for parents and students to work together to achieve success in school. It contains:

1. Messages that parents need to give their children about the importance of education.
2. Advice on how to engage in effective job planning:
   a. Encouraging students to start thinking about their future occupation.
   b. Motivating students to make their dreams become a reality.
3. Specific guidance for students that will help them improve their grades:
   a. How to master the basic skills, such as how to read books more effectively, strategies for taking different types of tests, and how to write an excellent term paper.
   b. A proven ten-point study system that shows students how to take the right subjects, get the most from their classes, prepare homework assignments, study for tests, and make the highest marks on tests.
   c. How to develop good study habits and still have plenty of time left over for other activities.

1

For Parents
and Students

The Importance of Education

How a Good Education and Good Job Translate into a Good Life

(It's the only life you have, and you are the one who will have to live it)

The ancient Greek philosopher Plato said, "The direction in which education starts a man will determine his future life." Truer words have never been spoken.

Students often have difficulty understanding the crucial importance of education in determining their future lives because they have not lived long enough to understand how the world really works. Reading books in various subjects in school is a good primer that increases understanding, but there is no substitute for living life and experiencing lessons personally, and this only comes with age. Parents already have been through many of the lessons in life, and they try to help their children get on the right track early and avoid many of the detours that lead in the wrong direction. In most cases, parents dispense their advice about the importance of education in an ongoing lecture, emphasizing different factors at different times on different occasions. All too often students are of the impression that they have heard this lecture before, and the advice is rarely heeded. A more useful approach is to have a *thorough* discussion about the importance of education at a single sitting, with additional reinforcement dispensed periodically to emphasize the validity of the lesson. One of my father's favorite sayings was, "You cannot put an old head on young shoulders," and that may very well be the case, but we are going to attempt to go a long way in that direction!

In this chapter I present a good, hard dose of reality about the importance of education in today's world that parents and students can discuss with each other. I start off by describing how life in the United States used to be, and then how it has changed through various demographic, social, and economic changes that have taken place during the past several decades. Next, I describe two possible scenarios, one that applies to people who do not obtain higher education and one that applies to people who do obtain it. Then I talk about the importance of where one lives, for both comfort and future success, and how a good education and good job provide the freedom that allows people to choose where they want to live. I present a strategy that parents can use to drive these points home to their students. Finally, I close with some statistics that show how earnings and wealth vary with different levels of education.

Changes that Have Occurred in the United States

The demographic, social, and economic changes in the United States that I will discuss encompass six areas: (1) changes in family structure, (2) changes in the age structure of the population, (3) changes in the racial and ethnic composition of the population, (4) changes in the return to education and skills, (5) changes in the structure of the economy, and (6) changes in the geographical location where goods and services are produced. As you will see, each of these changes has resulted in greater earnings and income inequality in the United States, and a more competitive world that students will face upon completing school.

Changes in Family Structure

When I was growing up in the 1950s and '60s, family types and living arrangements were quite standard. Most families were married couples with children, with a husband being the sole breadwinner and the wife staying home to take care of the home and family. Over the next couple of decades, many women entered the labor force and continued to work even with small children, dropping out of the workforce for only a short period of time to have their children. There were large increases in the incidence of divorce and separation, and the number of families headed by women and their children continued to grow. Many of these women had little prior work experience and thus were not able to command good salaries in the workforce. Many with young children and additional home responsibilities found it difficult to work at all and ended up in poverty.

At the same time, the families with a working husband and working wife now had two earners in the family, and their incomes grew significantly. These changes in family structure led to increased inequality of family income, with many families with working husbands and working wives clustering at the upper end of the income distribution, versus many female-headed families clustering at the lower end of the distribution.

Changes in the Age Structure of the Population

The basic demography of the population in terms of what is called the population profile began to change with the aging of the baby boom generation. The baby boomers are the roughly seventy-eight million people who were born in the United States during the two decades (1946 to 1964) following World War II, a phenomenon that took place in many other developed countries as well. The aging of the baby boomers has had an enormous influence on the job market and the types of goods demanded in our society. Just think about the adjustments that occurred as these people entered the labor market during the late 1960s through the early 1980s, demanded more housing and purchased more of the goods needed by children as they married and formed families during the latter quarter of the twentieth century, and what will happen during the twenty-first century as they age and demand more medical care and put a strain on retirement systems such as Social Security.

The relevant point for this discussion is the often-overlooked fact that inequality is higher among older generations than among younger ones, especially when wealth is taken into account, because the former have had a whole lifetime to practice behavior that leads to higher inequality. Some older person are barely scraping by on Social Security payments, while others have substantial income from pensions and sizeable asset holdings, such as a home that is fully owned. In addition, life expectancy increased at the same time that birth rates decreased, so more of baby boomers are still alive and will remain alive, and there will be fewer people to support them in their old age. As the baby boom generation ages and remains a large segment of the population, this will increase the overall level of inequality in our society.

Changes in the Racial and Ethnic Composition of the Population

The basic racial and ethnic composition of the American population has changed dramatically since the middle of the twentieth century. Groups that historically have had much higher birth rates but lower levels of income, such as blacks and Hispanics, have become a much larger percentage of the population. At the same time, minority groups that have incomes as high as or higher than whites, such as Asians, have also become a larger proportion of the population. These trends have been compounded by the increasing immigration of minority groups such as Hispanics into the United States, both those who are here legally and those who are here illegally. Many recent immigrants have low levels of education and skill, and thus cluster at the lower end of the earnings distribution. Many illegal immigrants have difficulties finding jobs because of laws that prohibit their hiring, and thus work in jobs that pay even lower wages.

Immigrants from all over the world migrate to the United States, making America what Ben Wattenberg, my good friend and colleague at the America Enterprise Institute for Public Policy Research, referred to in a recent book as *The First Universal Nation*. Changes in the racial and ethnic makeup of the United States population have also tended to increase income inequality.

Changes in the Return to Education and Skills

Another area that has seen significant change over the past several decades is the role of education. Higher education has always been an important consideration in getting a good job, but in the 1950s and '60s many jobs did not require a college education and it was possible to advance up the job ladder without one. Things changed over time as more and more people, men and women alike, began going to college and majoring in fields that required technical and scientific knowledge. This was in response to the creation of jobs in these areas, as science and computer technology became more important in our economy. Women began to major in fields that were previously dominated by men, and there are now more women than men in college.

For many jobs in which a bachelor's degree was previously considered to be adequate, the changing nature of work demanded more formal training and the best jobs went to people with specialized training or advanced graduate level work. There was a large increase in the return to education, as people with advanced education began to earn much higher salaries than did those without such training. There was also a phenomenon that economists referred to as the return to "skill-biased technological change," and salaries increased tremendously for people who had the sophisticated technical skills that employers demanded, especially when faced with a shortage of such workers. These developments tended to increase the degree of earnings inequality among workers in the economy.

Changes in the Structure of the Economy

At the same time, the structure of the economy was undergoing fundamental change, along with the types of jobs created to meet this new reality. Manufacturing and heavy industry shrank and the number of service jobs increased dramatically, and the United States was referred to as a "service-based" economy. Some of these service jobs were in lower-paying fields, such as fast-food restaurant workers as well as various forms of personal services, as working people had less and less time to devote to these activities on their own. But some of the service jobs were in very high-paying fields such as law and medicine, as the changing nature of the economy and basic demography of the population generated an increase in these types of jobs.

The manufacturing sector has long been considered to be the mainstay of the middle class in America, but it seems to have thinned out to some degree. As manufacturing jobs disappeared, many of the people working in this area who had little education were forced to go into the relatively lower-paying service jobs. At the same time, people who had higher levels of education went into many of the higher-paying service jobs. These trends have tended to increase the degree of earnings inequality as people with less education clustered at the lower end of the distribution, and people with higher education clustered at the upper end of the distribution.

Changes in the Geographical Location where Goods and Services Are Produced

In case you are wondering what happened to many of the higher-paying manufacturing jobs that no longer exist in the United States economy, many were exported to other countries that have lower wage structures. Whether one is talking about shoes, clothing, cars, or the production of industrial equipment, other countries with a workforce that will work for less can produce these products and ship them for less than it would cost to produce them in the United States, forcing companies to shift the location of production to remain competitive. And, more recently, it is not only the manufacturing jobs that have been exported. Many technical jobs, such as those involving computer science occupations, have been exported to countries such as India that have the technical expertise and can perform them more cost effectively.

The American worker must now be concerned not only with competition from other workers in his or her own city or nation, but from other nations around the world. The growth of huge multinational organizations has accelerated these trends, which will likely increase in the future. These trends toward globalization have also increased the degree of earnings inequality in our society.

The Bottom Line: More Inequality

The net result of all of these trends is to increase earnings and income inequality, and to make the world a more competitive place. The way economists generally measure the degree of income inequality is with the Gini index, named after Italian statistician Corrado Gini. The Gini index is a statistical measure that varies from zero (perfect equality) to one (perfect inequality). Thus, if everyone had the same income, the Gini index would be zero; and if one person had all of the income and no one else had any, the Gini index would be one. The higher the Gini index, the greater the degree of income inequality. According to the U.S. Census Bureau, between 1968 and 2007 the Gini index for household income increased from 0.386 to 0.463. This may not sound like a very large increase, but a trained economist would tell you that it is huge. Statistically speaking, there is no question that income inequality has increased dramatically in the United States over the past several decades.

It is important to understand that income inequality is increasing not because of some sinister or malevolent force, but because of the decisions that people make in a free society. For example, as more people decide to obtain higher education and move into higher-paying occupations, income inequality increases. The United States has always had a large middle class, which many say is the bastion of our stability, and probably it will always be. However, workers will increasingly face stiff competition from all quarters, and they will need to have high levels of education to compete effectively so they can maintain or enhance their standard of living in this country. Higher education was important before, but it has now become more important than ever before. As my landlord when I was a college student used to say, "It's every man for himself and the devil take the hindmost!"

Two Scenarios: Low Education and High Education

What I will do now is sketch out two scenarios, one that refers to what someone without much education can expect from the labor market and our society, and the other what someone with high levels of education and training can expect.

People who do not have much education in today's world will likely face a lifetime of struggle both in their jobs and their home life. Rather than being able to choose the occupation of their dreams, they will likely end up in a job that no one else wants. Jobs that require low education usually have low pay, unpleasant working conditions, irregular working hours, lack of intellectual stimulation, few fringe benefits, and poor opportunities for advancement. Because just about anyone can do these jobs, there is little likelihood that wages or working conditions will improve in the future. The longer people stay in such jobs, the smaller the chance they will ever escape, unless they obtain additional education and training. People who get involved in work that requires heavy physical labor often cannot work as long as others in more pleasant working conditions because of the stress and strain on their body. And when they collect their paycheck at the end of the week, they find that they cannot afford all of the things they would like to buy. They will not be able to buy the type of house they want in the neighborhood where they want to live, as well as the car they want or all of the other things that go along with it.

I do not want to sound too materialistic, but life is a continual struggle for people who do not have enough money, and they often have to forego basic necessities such as health care. Such people often go deeply into debt. If their credit worthiness deteriorates, they will have to pay higher interest rates for the money they borrow, and they will never be able to save and get ahead. The situation does not get any easier for children who grow up in such surroundings. Not only is there never enough money to buy the things they want, they will likely have to go into debt with a hefty education loan just to escape the situation. The situation often repeats generation after generation, unless someone has the good fortune to break out of it.

Contrast this pessimistic scenario with the more optimistic one for people who have obtained a substantial amount of education. Rather than having to take whatever job is available, they will move into an occupation that requires technical knowledge or professional skills. Such jobs usually have high pay, pleasant working conditions, extensive intellectual stimulation, good fringe benefits, and excellent opportunities for advancement. People who have extensive education often end up in a career in which they identify with the mission of a profession and the people who practice it. They enjoy going to work every day and making a significant contribution to society. If the economy takes a turn for the worse, or the company they work for has financial misfortune, they can usually recover quickly with another organization because of their extensive education and experience. People involved in professional careers are often rewarded handsomely with a substantial paycheck, which gives them the freedom to live in the house they want in the neighborhood where they want to live, with the car they want and all of the other things that go along with it.

And again, although it may sound like I am being materialistic, the point I want to make is that what money really buys is *freedom*—the freedom to have these things or not have these things, but most important, the freedom to choose.

People who make a substantial amount of money, if they are wise, save and invest and see their assets grow rather than going into debt. Having money is almost like having another worker in the house, because money invested will earn a good return. The more you have in money and other assets, the easier it is to make them grow. With substantial funds, there is the opportunity to enjoy nice things, take interesting vacations, and send children to the best schools, without having them go into debt. And like the more dismal scenario I sketched out earlier, the situation repeats generation after generation, except this time it is heading in the right direction.

The Importance of Location

Earlier I mentioned that a substantial income provides the opportunity for people to buy the house they want in the neighborhood where they want to live. It used to be that the "big three" factors for success were the right job, the right spouse, and, of course, one's health. To these three factors must now be added the location where one lives. Realtors always say that the three most important factors about a house are "location, location, location." These three factors must now be raised by an exponent because location is now more important than it has ever been before.

What is happening, not just in the United States but around the world, is that smart, highly educated persons are locating in certain megalopolises, for lack of a better word. In the United States, you will find highly educated people in the metropolitan areas of New York, Washington, D.C., Chicago, San Francisco, and Los Angeles. Overseas concentrations can be found around areas in London, Paris, Berlin, Tokyo, and Beijing. In these areas in the United States there are numerous opportunities for high-paying jobs that require advanced education. People want to locate in the best areas within these metropolitan areas, where there are excellent public schools to educate their children. Because of the proximity to good jobs and good schools, the property values of homes in these desirable areas have skyrocketed, far beyond what it cost to build them. If a home in these areas has other desirable features, such as plenty of land, good-quality construction, and nearness to conveniences, it is worth even more.

The reason that location has become so important is that one has to live in and around these areas to take advantage of the job opportunities and opportunities to educate their youth. For most Americans, the vast majority of their wealth is in their home, and people who live in these areas are making the best investment they can because their wealth will grow much faster than in a sluggish area.

Assortative Mating

There is another reason why where one lives is so important, and it is the little-known concept of "assortative mating," which is derived from the study of evolution. Simply put, people with similar characteristics tend to marry each other. Our youth may think that there is one unique person in the world who is ideally suited for them, and with new technology such as computer matching there is an increased likelihood that they will find that one person, wherever they are located. Well, the truth of the matter is that people tend to select mates from the areas where they live, go to school, and work. After all, this is where they are most likely to meet members of the opposite sex.

Now you can see why where one lives is so important, because this is where people with similar education, background, and values tend to locate. Sure, there are differences and the old adage is that "opposites attract," but increasingly in today's world people tend to marry other people with similar levels of education, because they are looking for compatible partners. "Lady and the Tramp" is a charming childhood parable, but the simple truth of the matter is that there are not many ladies out there looking for tramps!

The union of highly educated men and women in marriage has been driving up income inequality in the United States. Large numbers of women in college today are studying the fields traditionally chosen by men, and they are going into the labor force in record numbers and making the commitment to work full time over their lifetime. When a highly educated husband and highly educated wife are married and working full time, they generate a very high family income, especially as they age and move up the job ladder. These are the people who can afford to pay the high prices of homes in the desirable areas, and their willingness to do so bids the price far above what many other people can afford to pay. One of the reasons that earnings and income inequality has grown so rapidly in the United States is that there are more and more people who are in this category.

A Good, Hard Dose of Reality

There is another old adage that "seeing is believing." I do not want to appear crass, but one of the best ways for parents to give students a good, hard dose of reality is to let them see what money buys, all the while emphasizing that a good education is what is likely to generate money. For example, parents can take students on a family field trip in which they drive through the best and worst neighborhoods in their area. Parents should show their children firsthand what it is like to live in a neighborhood in which the people do not have much money, where the buildings are old and rundown, where living conditions are cramped, where there is graffiti on the walls, people drinking liquor out of a bag or selling drugs on the street, and where it is not safe to go to school or walk down the street at any time. Then parents should ask their children the question: "Is this where you want to end up? Because if you do not have a good education and good job, you might be the next new tenant."

Driving through impoverished neighborhoods does not teach the full extent of the lesson. Students should be encouraged to volunteer their time and effort to help improve the conditions in these areas. There are any number of nonprofit organizations that devote their efforts to cleaning up such neighborhoods and helping the residents who live in them. For example, I have volunteered to help a nonprofit organization that delivers food to needy and ill people, many of whom live in substandard housing. Volunteering will not only help students understand how difficult it is for people without much money to get by, it will make a difference in their lives and improve conditions in the community.

Next, parents should take their children for a drive through the most expensive neighborhood they can find in their metropolitan area. They should point out the sumptuous homes with extensive acreage, well-kept grounds, and recreational areas such as personal tennis courts and swimming pools. It is worth noting that there is plenty of room and no questionable or criminal activity taking place in the street. Parents should then drive to nearby areas and observe the availability of shopping centers, upscale stores, and impressive business establishments. Such arrangements are likely to occur together because good areas are usually well zoned. The important lesson is that the way one affords to live in such a neighborhood is to obtain a good education and go into a profession. Parents should then ask their children the question: "Would you rather live here or in the neighborhood we just visited? Because if you start applying yourself in school then this is a possibility." Crass perhaps, but it helps to drive the point home!

If "seeing is believing," then "experiencing is convincing." There is no better way for parents to convince their students of the importance of education than to have them work in a boring, or even grueling, summer job that pays meager wages. In the next chapter I will relate my experience of working at a summer job in a cinder block factory during my high school years. If parents can find a job this unpleasant for their children, I guarantee that it will be a wonderful eye-opener, and will change their attitude toward school when the fall term starts. Alternatively, if students find a job that requires long or irregular hours, boring and monotonous work, tiring physical labor, and near-starvation wages, this will have a similar effect. One does not have to look far for such a job in our economy because there are plenty of them and no one else wants to take them.

Aside from the purpose that I have recommended, a summer job is a wonderful learning experience, a way to include prior work experience on a résumé, and a way to earn extra income to cover educational expenses. My attitude is that everyone should be working all of the time, and too many summers are wasted by students doing frivolous, nonproductive activities. Sure, they need a break after spending most of the year in school, but are three months necessary? How about a couple of weeks of summer vacation, and then off to the "salt mines" like the rest of us? It is one of the best investments they will ever make!

Education and Earnings Data

I am going to close this chapter with a more direct discussion of the benefits that education brings in terms of a higher income, based on data from the U.S. Census Bureau. For many years, I directed the office that produces these statistics, so I am very familiar with their inherent message. I suggest that parents and students both look very closely at table 1 because it drives home the strong relationship between education and earnings. The table shows mean annual earnings by various levels of educational attainment for men and women. I have chosen to present mean earnings rather than median earnings because the U.S. Census Bureau's statistical tables on educational attainment show a maximum value of $100,000 for median earnings, which disguises the true income level of the higher paying educational categories. Although the dollar figures will become less relevant as this edition of the book ages, I encourage you to focus on the statistics that show the ratio of mean earnings in each educational attainment category to the overall average, because these relationships tend to remain more stable over time.

Table 1 provides a convenient means for ranking the various educational attainment categories by the level of earnings for men and women twenty-five years old and over who worked year round full time. In 2007, the overall mean earnings for year-round, full-time workers in all educational categories was $61,009 for men and $43,622 for women. The ratios in table 1 show how the earnings in a given educational attainment category compare to the overall average. Ratios greater than 1 indicate that people in the educational attainment category earn more than the overall average, and ratios less than 1 indicate that people in the educational attainment category earn less than the overall average. Although women tend to earn less than men in a given educational attainment category, the ratios shown for the various educational attainment categories are quite similar for men and women up through the high school degree level, but are lower for women than for men having a bachelor's degree or higher.

The major finding that stands out in table 1 is that people

with higher levels of educational attainment have higher earnings levels than do people with lower levels of educational attainment. Men with professional degrees, such as doctors and lawyers, earn about two and a half times more than the average for all men working year round full time, whereas comparable women earn about twice the overall average. People without a high school degree earn only about half as much as the overall average, and even those with a high school degree only earn less than three-fourths of the overall average. It may surprise you to learn that even people with an associate's degree (a two-year college degree) earn

Table 1. Mean Earnings in 2007 by Educational Attainment for Year-Round Full-Time Workers 25 Years Old and Over, by Sex

Educational Attainment	Men		Women	
	Mean Earnings	*Ratio to Total*	*Mean Earnings*	*Ratio to Total*
Total, all education levels	$61,009	1.00	$43,622	1.00
Less than 9th grade	$28,372	0.47	$21,355	0.49
9th to 12th grade, not high school graduate	$33,948	0.56	$22,717	0.52
High school graduate (including GED)	$44,016	0.72	$31,548	0.72
Some college, no degree	$51,923	0.85	$38,619	0.89
Associate's degree	$53,670	0.88	$42,093	0.96
Bachelor's degree	$79,018	1.30	$54,027	1.24
Master's degree	$94,919	1.56	$63,404	1.45
Doctorate degree	$117,629	1.93	$79,596	1.82
Professional degree	$154,320	2.53	$89,525	2.05

Source: U.S. Census Bureau, Current Population Survey, 2008 Annual Social and Economic Supplement.

less than the overall average. It is not until a person has a bachelor's degree that the average earnings level is about one-fourth higher than the overall average earnings level. A person who has a master's degree will earn about 50 percent more than the overall average, and someone with a doctorate will earn considerably more (see table 1).

These statistics should convince students of the very strong correlation between the level of educational attainment and earnings. The point should also be made that these statistics are overall averages, and some people will earn substantially more, whereas others will earn substantially less than the overall averages.

Education and Wealth

I noted earlier that there are even larger differences in wealth than in income for different educational groups, because people with more money have more opportunities to save and invest, and their wealth accumulates over time. Wealth statistics are not as plentiful as income statistics, but there is at least some information on wealth from the 2007 Survey of Consumer Finances conducted by the Federal Reserve Board and published in the *Federal Reserve Bulletin*. Wealth is measured as net worth, which is the difference between gross assets and liabilities. Unlike income, which represents a flow of money received over a period of time, such as a year, wealth is a stock concept showing what people are worth at a point in time. In other words, it shows how much they have accumulated over time.

The Survey of Consumer Finances indicates that families in which the head has a college degree on average have a net worth that is more than four times as high as families in which the head has a high school degree, a much larger difference than shown above for the earnings statistics. Moreover, families that own their own home on average have a net worth that is more than eleven times higher than the net worth of renters, which underscores my earlier point that a home is one of the most important assets a family can own. Parents should make sure that their children understand that the earnings differences shown above for a single year get magnified many times over during the course of a lifetime.

Conclusion

I have presented several arguments that parents can use to convince their children about the correlation between education and income, and why it is so important to get serious about school *now*. It is my hope that parents have had success in communicating these benefits to their students. However, words are only words to some, and it is often difficult to get a message across without actual experience. On the other hand, if students had the benefit of working in an unpleasant job during the summer, that was surely a convincing experience.

If parents are looking for additional ways to get the message across, then I offer the following strategy. Throughout my children's educational experience, I set up an incentive system to reward excellence in school and punish mediocrity. My strategy was that I paid my children $100 for each A (<u>A</u>ll right!) received in a course, nothing for a B (<u>B</u>ad!), and if they received a C (<u>C</u>atastrophe!) or lower in any course on their report card, then all bets were off and they received nothing, even if they earned A's in some courses. This system worked effectively for all of my children all through school.

You might call this bribery, but my rationale was that I was setting up a financial reward system much like they would encounter in the working world, so the approach would accomplish the intended objective while teaching an important lesson. Parents can easily do the same with their own children, and if they do not like the amounts or scale I used they can easily change them. The main point is that parents need to create some type of incentive structure for their students that encourages the proper attitude and behavior in school from the earliest years.

RECAP

Parents should establish the strong relationship between educational excellence and financial reward in their children's mind as early as possible. They should:

1. Make sure they understand the forces that are increasing income inequality.
2. Show them what money buys in terms of physical goods.
3. Encourage them to work in a "tough" summer job to learn what life is about.
4. Show them the statistics on how highly correlated education is with earnings.
5. Set up some type of incentive structure that produces the desired result.

Others Who Have Had Difficulty in School Have Succeeded

(Anything is possible if you put your mind to it)

Renowned British physician Havelock Ellis said, "It is on our failures that we base a new and different and better success." It is possible for students to perform at the highest level even if they have struggled with their studies in the past, especially if they can learn from their mistakes.

As I mentioned earlier, at different times of my life I have been one of the worst students imaginable and one of the best students imaginable. As you will see, my experiences were like a roller coaster. Although as a young student I was very diligent—some even said gifted—in high school everything fell apart completely. In college I started to work my way back, and it was not until graduate school that I realized my potential. When I tell my story to others, I find that they have gone through similar experiences, although sometimes in a different sequence or at different ages.

I remember how much I enjoyed school while a student in elementary and junior high (middle) school during the

late 1950s. I was very conscientious about listening to everything my teachers said in class, tried my hardest on classroom assignments, took all of my books home nightly, and
expended great effort in doing a good job on my homework.
At the time, I did not really know anything about how to
study (few schools teach these skills even today) so I accomplished my objectives by putting in a lot of hours of hard
work. My efforts were very successful: I received A's in just
about all of my courses, the teachers were very complimentary about my accomplishments (especially when they met
with my parents at PTA meetings), and my parents were very
happy with my progress. I took pride in my work and felt
gratified in the grades I received. Moreover, I had a genuine
interest in learning, because I was intellectually curious
about everything and spent large amounts of my leisure time
during holidays and summer vacations reading books of all
sorts.

By the time I entered high school, in the early 1960s,
everything began to fall apart rapidly. We had moved to a
new area quite a distance away, and I had to make all new
friends, which I think was the major source of my problems.
I fell in with a group of kids that were not bad in the sense
of being involved in drugs, alcohol, or crime, but they were
totally indifferent to school. My new associates were something akin to contemporary bodybuilders. All they cared
about was getting big and strong, and they lifted the heaviest
weights (even streetcar wheels) that they could find, ran ex-
cruciating distances at full speed, and took just about every
food supplement imaginable to accomplish their objective.
Believe me, they were much more concerned about finding
the largest all-you-can-eat buffet than with anything happening at school. I do not know why I fell in with them;
perhaps it was something captivating in their lifestyle. I was
a very scrawny kid at the time, and I could not believe the

changes in my body that resulted from following them—and other people took notice, which encouraged me even more!

Students in the same age bracket today fall in with many other kinds of groups (peer groups) that distract them from school and do a lot of harm. The great irony is that students join groups to establish their identity, yet in the process lose any identity they ever had.

Back to my story. Because my grades had been quite good in elementary school and junior high, the guidance counselors in my new high school had me tracked in the academic program with the brightest students. (I know the schools say that they do not track students, but just look around in your school and you will see that most of the brightest students are in the same classes, and vice versa.) The guidance counselors at my high school had no idea of my counterproductive lifestyle with the bodybuilders, so they signed me up for the heavy-duty academic classes, including advanced algebra, trigonometry, chemistry, physics, and foreign language. But now I was not listening to anything in class, not taking my books home in the evening, not doing my homework, and not even trying on the tests. It was a complete wipeout! I made D's (they were gifts) and F's in most of my classes. The only course in which I made straight A's was art class, because I was adept at drawing and oil painting. My English teacher gave me passing grades because I could write amusing stories.

As you might expect, my parents were devastated by my sudden academic decline. At first there was yelling, then there was crying, and then absolute frustration. They tried to get me away from my friends, who they realized were a bad influence on me, but that did not work, either. What I did not realize at the time, and what most students probably do not realize today, is that their academic success is a major concern to their parents. Most parents will do just about anything for their children, and the success of their children is more important to them than their jobs or anything else in their lives. Just ask parents what really matters to them and they will tell you that they are working for the well-being of their children. The feeling is probably biologically instinctive, in terms of perpetuation of the human species, and nothing matters more than one's own bloodline. If I had realized how much grief I was causing my parents at the time, that one factor alone probably would have caused me to alter my behavior.

My mother was particularly concerned about my situation, so she spoke to her boss, who was a real estate broker. "I know just what he needs," her boss said, "so you bring him in tomorrow morning to see me." My mother's boss did know exactly what I needed at the time, and he knew how to challenge me. I had just finished the eleventh grade, barely scraping by. It was the summertime, and I needed a job to earn some spending money. My mother's boss knew about the kids I was hanging around with, so he dared me to go to work for a friend of his who owned a local company. It was a cinder block factory, located in Forestville, Maryland. He said that it took a person of great strength to work in a cinder block factory and that it was much tougher than anything I or my friends had ever encountered, and that I probably would not be able to handle it. It was a challenge that I could not pass up, and probably the most significant turning point in my life.

It has been more than forty-five years since I took the summer job in that factory, but I remember the experience just as clearly as if it happened yesterday. I reported to work at 7:00 A.M. to a dingy gray building, surrounded by stacks of cinder blocks that gave it the impression of a malformed medieval castle. The owner, a crusty, tough old man carrying a cinder block in each hand, gave me one look and said, "Son, you're either gonna get real strong or you're gonna die!" He then told me that the pay was $1.05 an hour, that I could break periodically for water (as long as it was not too often), and that I could have about twenty minutes for lunch. The length of the workday was nine hours. He handed me a pair of neoprene (rubber) gloves, and said that they should last a couple of days.

As I walked over to the staging area in the hazy southern Maryland air laden with the morning's humidity, I soon realized what the experience was all about. My basic job was to unload and stack cinder blocks in square piles on a pallet as they came out of the oven in the dingy gray building. It was before the days of mechanization, so the hot cinder blocks had to be unloaded and stacked by hand. Without the neoprene gloves, the flesh on one's hands would have been sheared off in a matter of minutes. There was a whole gang of us in the staging area, mostly older men who had been at the factory for quite a while. The blocks came out of the ovens so quickly that by the time a whole tray was unloaded and stacked, another tray was just arriving. Hunching us over at the waist, the full nature of the job was to unload and stack the cinder blocks as quickly as possible. There was no waiting around or resting.

I find it difficult to describe in words the nature of the experience. As the morning's humidity wore off, the hot summer sun came burning down on the asphalt lot in the staging area, raising the temperature to well above one hundred degrees Fahrenheit. The heat from the freshly baked cinder blocks accentuated the experience, making me feel that I was also in the oven. After a few hours, the pain in my shoulders and forearms was screaming. Someone began to sing a rhythmical song and we all joined in, and I realized that the reason people on a chain gang sing is to forget about the pain. I did not know the words to most of the songs, but I soon learned them.

At midmorning on the first day, a loud bell rang and I thought through the sweat pouring off my brow that it was the Lord offering us a break. Instead I heard the stentorian voice of the straw boss: "Okay, men, let's load two thousand blocks on them flatbed trucks, *double time!*" After we loaded the trucks, we drove a few miles down the road to a construction site and unloaded two thousand blocks. I knew that I never wanted to hear the sound of a bell again. As we returned and I was staggering back to the staging area, one of the older men on the chain gang said to me with a wide smile, "You'd better get serious about your studies, son, or you're going to be back here with us in the fall!" Apparently, the news about me had preceded my arrival, and they were all having some fun.

On Saturday morning after the first week, my mother's boss stopped by my house to see how I was doing. I was still in bed, trying not to move in any direction so I would not feel any pain. "How's it going?" he said, extending his thick palm for a handshake. I told him about my experiences of the past week, and that the only thing missing was an iron ball and chain around my ankle. He laughed and laughed some more, until finally he had to sit down on the bed. "Well," he said, after finally composing himself, "you have a couple of days to rest up before you report back Monday morning. Don't forget our deal: I got you the job and I expect you to stick it out!"

I learned two important lessons from my summer job at the cinder block factory. First, I realized the connection between education and the world of work, and that without education all one could expect was the most menial type of job with unpleasant working conditions and very little pay. Second, the experience taught me the value of money, because whenever I spent any money it made me think of what I had to do to earn it.

To this day, whenever I have something unpleasant to do at a job, I think back to my first job, and everything else seems tame by comparison. The experience at the cinder block factory scared the living bejesus out of me because it made me realize that I had been on the wrong track for the past couple of years of my life, and that I needed to do something quickly to repair the situation. It was my *wake-up call!* All students should have an experience like mine, preferably at a young age when they can still do something about it.

In his epic work, *Paradise Lost*, English poet John Milton wrote, "Long is the way And hard, that out of hell leads up to light." His words were more relevant to my situation at the time than I realized.

When I returned to high school in my senior year, I was determined to do a better job on my studies. I wanted to go back to the days when I was an A student in elementary and junior high school, but I found it to be a difficult task. I had missed so much of the essential material for the past three years when I was goofing off, I did not know where to begin. It was impossible for me to go back and read all of the books on subjects I had failed, such as chemistry, physics, and trigonometry, so I focused on trying to learn the basics in English and mathematics that would help me with my courses in the twelfth grade. I did such things as reading the dictionary and writing down the meanings of words I did not know in a notebook, or going back to earlier books in mathematics to learn the fundamentals of algebra. I did not know the first thing about studying, so I tried to overcome my inadequacies with plenty of hard work, as I had done earlier.

I tried my hardest in my senior year and was able to improve my grades significantly, but I was not even close to being an A student. There is an important lesson here for other students who waste their time as I did: It is not so easy to come back when you have missed essential material in the curriculum, even if it is your greatest desire. However, because I was able to raise my grades, and colleges put the most emphasis on one's recent experience, the University of Maryland agreed to put me in a trial remedial program (precollege summer session) after I graduated from high school to see if I could be admitted as a freshman in the fall. In the early 1960s, the University of Maryland was not a competitive school as it is today, and just about any state resident was given a chance to enter, which is why I think they gave one to me. In the summer program I took two courses, Composition and American Literature, and American Government. The terms of the summer program were straightforward: If I received less than a C in either course, I would not be admitted in the fall. I broke my rear end with work, and regularly attended special reading and study skills classes, but I still did not know the basics of how to study. I barely scraped by with two C's.

When I entered the university as a full-time student in the fall of 1964, my experiences were not much different. I enrolled in seventeen credit hours of various introductory courses and again worked my tail off, but I still did not know how to study. I was trying to figure it out as I went along. At the end of the term my grades were pathetic: three C's, three D's, and a B in Composition and World Literature. The second semester was a little better, and I managed to make several B's, but still with a smattering of C's and D's. By my sophomore year I had settled on a major I liked, economics, because I felt that it helped me understand how the world of business and industry operated. I still did not have a systematic method of study, but my study habits improved somewhat and so did my grades. I even managed to make several A's in my major, although I was never able to earn above a 3.6 grade point average in any semester as an undergraduate.

By the time I had graduated from the University of

Maryland in 1968, I was like most other recent graduates: I wanted out of school fast so I could go into the working world. I found a job as an economist in the federal government, working for the U.S. Census Bureau. I had a brief stint in my career working at the U.S. Bureau of Labor and Statistics, but then I returned to the U.S. Census Bureau. After working a few years on income and poverty statistics, I decided that I wanted to go to graduate school in economics to expand my knowledge. I went to see a former professor for advice, and he gave me some sobering news. If I was serious about going to graduate school in economics, then I needed a much more extensive background in mathematics and statistics than what I had obtained as an undergraduate. As an undergraduate I had taken the bare minimum needed to graduate, mostly what are known as cookbook courses. My adviser told me that I should go through the mathematics and statistics series for scientists and engineers rather than being taught by economists, because most of them did not really understand these subjects. As you might imagine, this sent a shudder up my spine, especially since I had missed so many of the fundamentals in my earlier education.

Determinedly, I forged ahead with my study of mathematics and statistics. I enrolled as a part-time evening student at University College, part of the University of Maryland, while still working full-time during the day at the U.S. Census Bureau. It was a demanding program: several courses in differential and integral calculus, linear algebra, and mathematical statistics and probability. What made the program especially challenging for me was that most of the examples in the textbooks were from physics, the course that I had failed in high school.

I was more frightened than you might imagine, but resolved to see it through, so I approached my new task as an economist approaches problems. An economist, I reasoned, builds models to explain the behavior of the economy, so the first thing I was convinced of was that I needed to build an effective system of study, a skill no one had ever taught me. I broke each of the tasks down: what I needed to do to succeed in the classroom, what I needed to do at home to prepare for assignments and complete homework, what I needed to do to prepare adequately for examinations, and what I needed to do to earn the highest grades on those examinations. The rudimentary system of study that I developed surpassed my expectations. I made an A on every test, paper, and course that I took in mathematics and statistics. I was working hard as I had done before, but now with a systematic method of study that seemed to be foolproof.

The U.S. Census Bureau had provided financial support for the mathematics and statistics courses that I had taken, because they were work related. My boss took notice. It was a time of much exploratory and developmental work on the statistical measurement of poverty in our office, and my boss said that he needed someone who really understood the material. He made me an offer that I could not refuse. If I was willing to go to graduate school in economics, then the U.S. Census Bureau would pick up the expense for tuition and books, as long as all of the courses I took were work related. There was one catch: I had to work full-time and take all of the courses in the evening. Enthused by the prospect of learning new things that I could bring directly into the work at the office, and emboldened by my newly found success in taking mathematics and statistics courses, I agreed to the proposition.

My first task was to find a graduate school of economics in my area (the Washington, D.C., metropolitan area) for which one could attend the entire program in the evening. The only program at the time was at George Washington University, which also had a very good school of economics.

I applied and was accepted immediately into the Ph.D. program, bypassing the master's degree. They obviously overlooked my less-than-stellar grades as an undergraduate student and focused on my accomplishment in mathematics and statistics, which were essential for success in economics at the graduate level. The department even waived the standard requirement for mathematical statistics, although I went on to take several advanced courses in mathematical economics, econometrics, and operations research.

I was very confident that I would succeed in the Ph.D. program in economics at George Washington University, even though I was working full-time during the day, because of my success in taking mathematics and statistics courses. I continued to expand and refine the system of study I had developed, and applied it all through graduate school. The results again surpassed my expectations: I made an A on every test, paper, and course through the entire program—a straight 4.0! The courses I took and the grades I received are shown on my academic transcript in appendix D. And I accomplished this while working full-time at the U.S. Census Bureau and taking care of home and family responsibilities.

Other good things began to happen for me. I was placed in charge of direction of the nation's official statistics on income and poverty, and my responsibilities were expanded to include direction of all of the economic work in the Population Division at the U.S Census Bureau. In reality, I was actually working about fifty hours a week at my job and going to graduate school in the evening, where I made A's in all of my courses. My promotions at work reinforced the strong connection between advanced levels of education and occupational success.

There is another important advantage of working during the day and going to graduate school in the evening, which I soon realized. As part of the requirement of earning a Ph.D., students are expected to write an original dissertation that expands the field of knowledge. For my dissertation I chose the subject of earnings levels of job entrants by race and sex, and what happens to these earnings levels after workers have been in the labor force for ten years. For the empirical work on my dissertation, I used the official data on income distribution from the U.S. Census Bureau that I had helped to create. I remember when I was going in to defend my dissertation before a panel of six professors and the dean at the university, my adviser said to me, "You have a significant advantage here, because if they challenge your data, who do they have to consult? *You!*" I was very relaxed during the defense of my dissertation, because at the outset one of the professors jokingly remarked to his colleagues, "Gentlemen, the question is not whether Mr. Green will pass this test, but whether *we* will." The dissertation was accepted by the university and received much public attention. It was published on the front page of *The New York Times* (January 16, 1984), and I appeared on *CBS Morning News* to discuss the findings.

When you have worked so hard for so long, and everything comes to a halt when you finish your degree, you wonder what you are going to do next. My adviser told me that he asked the dean to give me a special award for making A's in everything, but the dean said that there was no such award because he did not know of anyone else who had done it. It was then that I started to feel that my foolproof system of study could be used to help others (including my own children!), so I decided to write everything down before I forgot it. After a while I had something that started to look like a book (my first), so I named it *Getting Straight A's* and sent it around to various publishers (over the transom) after I had completed my first draft. I did not receive one response, not even a polite (or impolite) rejection. I went to see my good friend, author Ben Wattenberg, at the American Enterprise Institute for Public Policy Research. We had met through my work at the U.S. Census Bureau. He explained to me that I needed a literary agent, because an author of a first book does not get much attention from publishers. Ben connected me with Harold Roth in New York City, who has been the agent for all of my books including the present one.

Having found my avocation, I have written several books on education. The first edition of *Getting Straight A's* was published by Lyle Stuart in 1985, and there are now more than 500,000 copies in print, including the revised edition, which was published in 1993. The book has been translated into Spanish, Polish, and Vietnamese, and is used by college and university students all over the world. I adapted these study methods so they would apply to students in high school and below in *How to Get Straight A's in School and Have Fun at the Same Time,* which was issued in 1999 by my current publisher, Tom Doherty Associates, LLC. This book for younger students has gone through numerous printings and is used by younger students all over the world. Several people whom I have never met have written testimonials on the Internet on how these books have helped them succeed in school and life, which I will cover shortly.

My turnaround as a student helped me advance in my career, which in turn has enabled me to help others become better students. At the U.S. Census Bureau, my Ph.D. in economics enabled me to direct the preparation of the nation's income and poverty statistics and to become a member of the president's Senior Executive Service as chief of the Governments Division. At the U.S. Census Bureau, I regularly conducted seminars on how to become a better student for employees who were attending college in the evening, for which I received a special meritorious award. The U.S. Census Bureau regularly sent me to elementary and secondary schools during working hours, to conduct seminars with younger students on how to improve their grades. At Independent Sector, where I was vice president of research, I conducted seminars on how to become a better student, for employees in the nonprofit sector who were attending college in the evening. At the American Enterprise Institute for Public Policy Research, I regularly conducted seminars for interns, many from the most prestigious colleges in the country. I have devoted a substantial amount of my time working with students at all levels, in all locations, and in groups and clubs of various affiliations, whenever I thought I could make a difference.

One of my most enjoyable appearances was when I returned to my alma mater, Surrattsville High School in Clinton, Maryland, to talk about the publication of my first book, *Getting Straight A's*. A local reporter who wrote an article on the occasion dragged out the caption from my high school year book: "Gordon Woodrow Green, Jr. 'Mr. Clean' . . . adept artist . . . famous for his caricatures . . . ambition: 18-inch biceps." The reporter went on to say that my favorite part of school was the bell signaling the end of the day, and if my classmates were asked who among them might write a book on how to make straight A's in school, few (*none!*) would have thought of me! My high school guidance counselor had told me that I was not college material, and that I should not even apply for college because it would be a waste of their time and mine.

Notwithstanding my guidance counselor's discouraging advice, I ended up devoting a significant portion of my life to the field of education. In addition to the six books I have authored and numerous seminars I have conducted, I have done an extensive amount of work in the area of education for the federal government. For the National Center for Education Statistics, which is part of the U.S. Department of Education, I served as both the chair and vice-chair of the National Forum on Education Statistics, a forum comprised of leading education officials from all the states in the nation. This is the most important and influential forum in the country on elementary and secondary education statistics.

As a father, I have been very gratified that all three of my children followed my study system and graduated from college with excellent grades. I told each of them about my experiences as a youngster, and I was determined that they would not repeat the same mistakes I had made. My youngest child, Chris Green, was a valedictorian at Fairfax High School in Fairfax, Virginia, while playing on the school baseball team each year, and managed to graduate summa cum laude from the College of William and Mary with a 3.9 average. My middle child, Dana Green, graduated cum laude from George Mason University, despite the fact that she has a hearing loss and attention-deficit/hyperactivity disorder (ADHD). And my oldest child, Heidi, also graduated from George Mason University with an excellent scholastic record, and has gone on to a career of helping autistic children. In fact, Heidi's husband, Raphael Riemenschneider, who immigrated to the United States from Germany, has been taking college courses during the evening at George Mason University while working at a full-time job during the day, and he has managed to make mostly A's by following my system of study.

As a father, I can tell you that my life has been made easier and more enjoyable because of the success of my children in school. But you, as a reader, are certainly entitled to some evidence that these study methods work for more people than just the relatives of the author.

For that evidence, I refer you to the reviews of my first book, *Getting Straight A's,* on the Amazon.com Web site by the many people who have used my study methods over the years. I know very few of these people, but they have been inspired to write reviews to tell others about their success, and many of the stories are truly inspiring and heartwarming. There are stories of students who were on academic probation and who were totally overwhelmed by school, who followed my study methods and became A students. Other students say they were working at full-time jobs and attending night classes for years, spending hours studying each night and worrying about tests, before putting my study system into practice and succeeding. One student had struggled with low grades and barely graduated from high school, spending years afterward working in low-paying jobs, before putting my study system into practice in college and making straight A's semester after semester. One student even became a successful physician using my study methods, after being told by his high school guidance counselor that he should go into television or radio repair.

With all of my effort to help students, I received some sobering advice from a friend who is a well-known educator. He told me that he had no doubt that my study methods were effective, but my greatest challenge was to win the hearts and minds of younger students, to convince them that all of the effort needed to become a better student was worthwhile. That is the major reason that I have written this book.

There are three things that I hope you obtained from this chapter.

First, it is worthwhile to become a serious student and make the highest grades possible. This will enable students to have fuller lives by understanding more of what is happening in the world, obtaining the occupation of their dreams, and earning a high income that makes it possible to live in the style they desire. I present the full weight of my argument in the remaining chapters of part 1.

Second, my experiences as a student and the experiences

of others who have used my study methods should convince you that almost anything is possible. There is one important caveat, however, as illustrated by my experiences. The more basic material a student misses in the early years, and the longer he or she waits to turn things around, the more difficult the task will become.

Third, there are proven methods of becoming a better student, techniques that will enable one to accomplish more than ever thought possible. Remember, when I received a perfect record getting my Ph.D. in economics, I was working about fifty hours a week at a full-time job. If I can do it, so can other students! I will be teaching the secrets of these study methods in part 2.

RECAP

Other students with difficulties in school have succeeded.

1. **It is never too late to become a good student, regardless of the past.**
2. **However, the longer a student waits, the more difficult the task.**

3

The Beauty of Knowledge

(What you learn in school you will actually use later on)

English scientist and philosopher Sir Francis Bacon observed, "For all knowledge and wonder (which is the seed of knowledge) is an impression of pleasure in itself." Many people want knowledge for pragmatic purposes, but Bacon knew its true value.

Knowledge is a beautiful and pleasurable commodity, but this basic truism is not recognized by many young students in school. In fact, I have heard many students complain that they should not have to study a particular subject because they will never need to use the information again for the rest of their lives. Many students think only of the grind of attending school day in and day out, studying subjects in which they have no interest, and being forced to do homework and take tests on subjects they abhor. They often come into a course with a strong dislike of a subject, particularly if it seems difficult to learn or irrelevant to their everyday concerns. It is only a small step to start disliking teachers, the school, and the entire educational experience. For many students, the daily act of attending school and doing assignments is like a torture chamber, because they cannot see beyond the immediate work to the broader goals of what they are accomplishing. The great irony is that this attitude prevents students from enjoying the beauty and pleasure of knowledge in its own right, and their grades reflect it.

The job of parents in motivating students will be made easier by convincing them that knowledge is a joy to obtain, and it plays a significant role in shaping our identity. I find it useful to get students to think about the human experience and what it entails. We come into this world as infants without a shred of knowledge, and our minds are a blank slate, a tabula rasa, as ancient Greek philosopher Aristotle and others who followed him have noted. All we have is our genetic instincts and predispositions, but with a tremendous capacity to learn. The process begins early, as we learn to walk and talk and master the basics of life taught to us by our parents. But our parents can take us only so far, as only a few are trained educators and most do not have broad knowledge of subjects beyond their immediate areas of expertise. Parents should explain to their children that the whole purpose of education is to fill that blank slate with information that will help them understand the ways of the world (and the universe) and to function more effectively as they mature.

To motivate a desire for knowledge in young minds, I start with that important word "wonder" used by Francis Bacon. From the moment we come to consciousness, we are struck by wonder about our new surroundings. Regardless of their religious beliefs, people of all persuasions are filled with wonder about the miracle of existence itself. While scientists can tell us approximately when the universe started, none can tell us exactly how it started, other than speculating that it originated in a fraction of a second from a tiny singularity about the size of a dime. And yet, here we are, fifteen billion years or so later, a tiny piece of existence in that fragile structure that we call the human body, aware of our surroundings and capable with study of explaining how they operate according to the laws of nature. Moreover, scientists tell us that the heavier chemical elements in our body could only have been forged inside the cores of massive stars, where temperatures and pressures were great enough to create them. When these massive stars exploded in a supernova, the heavier chemical elements were spread around the universe, and eventually found their way into the human body.

Who wouldn't be interested in acquiring knowledge when confronted with such reality? We cannot explain how we got here, but we should be interested in finding out everything about what it entails. And yet, many students ignore the miracle of existence and concentrate only on the bureaucratic methods we have devised for imparting knowledge in our educational system. If parents encourage their children to stand back from the daily flurry of activity in the educational world and take a clear look at what existence is all about, I think they will find that it develops a thirst for knowledge for its own sake.

Humans have a natural curiosity to learn everything possible about their environment. If you have ever watched a young child at play in a sandbox, experimenting with different toys and artistic configurations made in the sand, you know exactly what I mean. No adult or educator needs to be present to foster the process. The child merely goes about progressive learning in his or her own way, experimenting with the various implements at hand, all the while deriving tremendous enjoyment from the experience. It is only when we yank young children out of the sandbox, often against their will, and put them into a structured learning environment, that problems start to arise. We disrupt their play, usually without even explaining why, other than to say that it is now time to go to school. Then, when they enter school, children are told what they can and cannot do, and the freedom of the sandbox seems lost.

When a child first enters school, the most important thing a parent can do is to explain that school will be fun and is just the continuation of the learning process from the sandbox. One can only be happy in a sandbox for a certain amount of time, until one has mastered just about everything that can be done in that environment. The child needs new and more challenging experiences, and the structure of school provides that setting, where experts can develop learning along various dimensions.

It is an irony that children do not really understand what their parents mean when they tell them that school is the "best time of their life." Adults can appreciate the truth of the statement because they have a basis for comparison. Adults quickly learn that to be paid a good salary, they need to become an expert within their field. And the mastery of unique skills brings a certain pleasure in its own right. But adults generally are not able to study a wide variety of interesting subjects in their jobs as children are able to study in school, without the various responsibilities of adulthood.

It is important for parents to instill in their children the great privilege of being able to be a generalist in the widest possible sense of the word. In school there is the opportunity to learn English, so we can understand others more effectively and develop the tools we need to acquire even more knowledge. With history we learn about the development of institutions and culture and scientific progress, for the country in which we live, or other countries around the world. We complement history with the social sciences, with economics to understand how the economy performs, with sociology to learn how people behave, and with anthropology to understand how cultures develop. With mathematics we learn the laws, relationships, and techniques to understand not only the quantitative aspect of things, but to manipulate the physical world around us. Mathematics is the handmaiden for understanding science, the basis for the existence of all things, from biology to chemistry to physics and the more specialized scientific disciplines. With philosophy, which is the foundation and basis of all knowledge, we gain the ability to stand back from everything to question and try to understand what it all means.

Many if not most of the things that students learn in school will be very useful to them later on. Yet to many students, learning the rigors of a discipline is viewed as a temporary task, to be forgotten as soon as an assignment is turned in or a grade has been received. Because children do not know the ways of the world, it is very difficult for them to imagine that anything learned in school has any practical relevance whatsoever.

What is learned in school will help the student to function effectively as a human being on the most basic level. The vocabulary and grammar learned in English courses plays an enormous role in how we express ourselves to others, whether in conversation with relatives, friends, or someone at a local store. Our speech says a lot about what we know, what we value, how effectively we can communicate our feelings, and who we are. A knowledge of mathematics is essential for understanding the more challenging disciplines in school, but it is also essential for functioning at the most basic level such as buying something in a store and getting back the right change, or being able to balance a checkbook. It is true that as technology advances we are freed from doing many of the mundane things people had to do in the past, but without a basic understanding of English and mathematics it becomes more difficult to function in our increasingly complex world. That is why many foreigners without a good understanding of the English language have so much difficulty functioning initially when they first arrive in the United States.

Let's take the discussion about the importance of mastering English and mathematics even further, as it relates to other courses in school. If one truly masters these two subjects, then all other subjects in school will be comparatively easier to learn. English is, of course, necessary for understanding all subjects in school, but it is especially important in understanding the social sciences, such as history, economics, sociology, psychology, anthropology, and government and politics. Mathematics is especially important in understanding the physical sciences such as chemistry and physics; and although we do not normally think of mathematics as being as important in other sciences such as biology, botany, and geology, at the higher levels of study it becomes very important in certain courses within these fields.

A student who has not mastered English and mathematics in high school will have a hard time mastering these other courses in the social and physical sciences in the high school curriculum, and even more difficulty when taking these courses at the college level. *All knowledge builds on a foundation, and if the foundation is weak then the entire structure may collapse.* The beauty of knowledge is that everything new builds on whatever has already been learned, which enhances its enjoyment and viability.

To appreciate the practicality of things learned in school for use later on, one needs to think about any number of occupations that one may assume after completing school, and the skills that are required to be successful in them. For example, if someone wants to become a real estate salesperson, specialized training will be acquired when entering the field, but all of the knowledge learned in English, social studies, and mathematics will be useful for understanding the basic concepts of real estate and communicating them to prospective clients. If someone wants to become a medical doctor, then all of the information learned in chemistry and biology will be especially important, not only for preparation to enter and succeed in medical school, but also in the practice of being a physician. In fact, all of the knowledge learned in English, social studies, and mathematics will also be important for the physician to speak in clear language, understand the needs of people, and be able to run a medical business effectively. In fact, to run any type of business effectively, the owner should have strong language skills and some knowledge of social studies and mathematics.

The real beauty of knowledge is that it gives us the ability to enjoy life more fully. A visit to the zoo is so much more interesting if you know the technical names of the various species of animals, how they evolved, and how they relate to one another and their natural habitat. (That is why all of this useful information is usually described on signs next to the viewing area.) A visit to the National Museum of Natural History at the Smithsonian Institution in Washington, D.C., will put the visit to the zoo in much broader and more interesting perspective. Viewing the flight of an airplane in the sky is so much more exhilarating if you understand the principle of lift and other aerodynamic concepts. Again, this is put into broader and more interesting perspective if you ever had the opportunity to visit the National Air and Space Museum at the Smithsonian Institution in Washington, D.C., to learn about the evolution of flight.

Even everyday experiences become more interesting if you understand the processes that underlie them. For example, driving in a rural area might reveal an excavation of the ground with various layers of rock exposed. How much more interesting the experience will be if you know the differences between igneous and sedimentary rocks, and the geological processes that produce them, rather than just observing that there is a large hole in the ground. And again, how much more interesting the perspective will be if you ever had the opportunity to visit the Grand Canyon National Park in Arizona, where you can observe the various layers of sandstone, shale, and limestone that were formed over the eons of geologic history. The capacity to enjoy life itself is very much a function of the knowledge that we possess.

If a child has a love of knowledge, then any form of learning and school itself will be welcomed as an enjoyable activity. Parents play a major role in developing the love of knowledge. It starts with the youngest years, with reading regularly to a child so he or she will develop a love of words and thoughts. It continues when the child is old enough to hold the book him- or herself, even though the words may not be understandable and pictures must be relied upon instead. And it continues when the child can read on his or her own, and will do so willingly with the provision of interest, encouragement, and reading material.

There are a number of specific activities that parents can do to stimulate their child's love of knowledge. Parents should take their child to the library, and show him or her the various sections of the stacks and what they contain. It is advisable to check out a number of different types of books from the library, and take the time to sit down and read and review them together. Once parents discover their child's predilection for a subject, they can encourage it by buying books, regularly or as gifts for special occasions or holidays. (Yes, I know it is expensive, but it is the best investment possible.) Parents can demonstrate their love of knowledge by reading on their own, perhaps when their child is also reading. There are quality programs on television, especially public television, in which knowledge is imparted along with the enhancement of pictures, but most of the programming is decidedly inferior and overconsumption of it should be discouraged. In general, children look up to their parents as role models, especially when they are very young, so parents should set a good example of the types of behavior that they want their children to practice.

Once a love of knowledge is developed in a child, the pursuit will normally progress on its own. The more knowledge children possess, and the more words they understand, the more readily they will pursue the acquisition of additional knowledge. In this regard, parents should encourage their child to reference a dictionary frequently when reading, and assist in explaining definitions if the meaning is unclear. One of the reasons some people have a strong dislike for learning is they do not have a good understanding of many words. If you are reading something you cannot really understand, it soon becomes very unpleasant.

Parents should encourage their child to look up the meaning of words in the dictionary, either in a book or online, and to understand the spelling, parts of speech, multiple meanings, and derivation of words. The child can even keep a small notebook of words that are difficult to understand, and through frequent reference the terms will become more familiar. The more words children know and understand, the easier and more enjoyable it will be to read additional material, and they will be anxious to learn new words to build their vocabulary. (Just think how much higher a student will score on the verbal portion of the SAT when this approach is followed all through school.) Students will start to develop a love of knowledge and reading on their own, and they will pursue the activity willingly.

One can tell when the pursuit of knowledge has developed fully, because children will then pursue it as a leisure activity. In other words, the activity becomes more strongly one of consumption rather than investment, although both elements are always present. In school, children do not have much of a choice of what to read because the reading materials are assigned, other than perhaps being given the choice of a novel to read and report on in English class. Thus, much of the time after school or even on the weekends during the school year will be preoccupied with doing readings for assignments, although some time will surely be left over. Children who still want to read after completing their assignments in school are pursuing reading as a leisure activity.

Parents should encourage their child to read materials of his or her own interest during these free times. If it comes down to a choice of whether to watch television and play video games or read a good book, less of the former and more of the latter is the preferred choice. However, a good schedule will always be balanced, like the "golden mean" of the ancient Greeks, so there should be some time allotted for sports and other activities in addition to reading for leisure.

During the summer months, when the school term is over, students have the opportunity to read a wide range of materials that suit their interest. Depending on their age, I strongly recommend reading some of the great classics of literature. So many books by so many authors are available today that one often does not know what to choose, but classic works by legendary authors are often the best choice. Some of my favorite authors are Ernest Hemingway, D. H. Lawrence, George Orwell, and Aldous Huxley, and I find that what they had to say dwarfs the message of many contemporary authors. If students like science fiction and fantasy, my current publisher (Tor and Forge Books), has a

wonderful selection of good novels for younger readers. Regardless of the subject, if a child truly recognizes the beauty
of knowledge, then reading good books will be more pleasurable than many competing activities. In appendix A, I have
included a suggested reading list prepared by the College
Board for college-bound students.

My love of knowledge has developed to such an extent
that I would like to sit down and read an entire encyclopedia
if I had the time. To many people, this would be a "nerdy"
thing to do because an encyclopedia is a reference source
used to look up detailed information on a subject you do not
understand. But to me, the encyclopedia is the repository of
all knowledge that represents what man has accumulated
over the ages. I have spent my entire lifetime studying various subjects, much of it for pure enjoyment, and to me it
would be a delight to sit down and read the entire encyclopedia from A to Z to supplement what I know with what I
missed.

So many subjects that we do not come into contact with
through a general education are fascinating in their own
right and affect our lives in ways that we do not understand.
Through reading widely about a vast array of subjects, we
begin to see the interrelationships between them and start
to understand how things really work. The broader your
knowledge base, the greater your capacity to enjoy all aspects of life, from the highly sophisticated to the essentially
mundane. That is the beauty of knowledge, and also the
spirit that should be communicated to students.

I have described the acquisition of knowledge thus far
through the medium of books, but knowledge is obtained in
many other ways as well. Parents can develop a love of knowledge in their child by using every experience from the earliest years as a learning moment. In particular, knowledge
can be used to explain how the world works. For example,

when shopping at the food store, parents can explain the various categories of foods, from what and where they are obtained, and how they fit into a healthy diet. This amounts to little more effort than talking during shopping. When driving by a factory on a trip, parents can explain what is produced there, what raw materials are used in the production process, how the product is used in conjunction with other goods and services, and whose needs it meets. Better yet, many factories allow tours during designated hours, so the explanations will be that much more meaningful if they occur during a tour. Before children go to the doctor for a checkup, they should be encouraged to look up easily understandable medical concepts in a book or on the Internet, and this will make the visit more interesting and perhaps even less frightening.

Parents should not miss the opportunity to take their child to work with them on special days designated by the government or their employer, so he or she will have the opportunity to learn more about what the parents do for a living. In fact, during any experience in which parents and children participate together, if parents take the time to describe their knowledge of what is happening, I think both will find the occasion more interesting and enjoyable.

The acquisition of knowledge is a continuous, lifelong experience. Although we normally think of a teacher as someone who imparts knowledge in a structured educational environment, in reality we are all teachers who impart knowledge in many different venues. Students with parents who take the task more seriously will have an advantage over those whose parents are indifferent, or who say that they are so busy that they do not have the time to spend with their children. Whatever parents' background or income level, if they transmit the right attitudes about knowledge and learning to their students, then half of the battle is

won. Students who love knowledge will not only study subjects willingly in school, but will view them as an opportunity to increase their lifelong knowledge base.

RECAP

**If parents teach their children to appreciate the beauty of
knowledge, then all other actions needed for success in
school will follow naturally:**

1. Obtaining knowledge is pleasurable in its own right.
2. Knowledge learned in school has great practical utility.
3. Expanded knowledge increases the ability to enjoy life.
4. Acquisition of knowledge is a continual, lifelong pursuit.

The Value of Getting Good Grades

(They build confidence and self-esteem, and expand opportunities)

Legendary American investor and businessman Warren Buffet said, "Value is what you get." As in the business world, the value of making good grades in school is what you get for achieving them!

The Dividends of Getting Good Grades

Getting good grades in school will provide many dividends to students, and parents should make sure that they are aware of them. The benefits of getting good grades in school include: (1) a feeling of confidence and self-esteem, (2) satisfaction for a job well done, (3) less stress at home with parents, (4) an opportunity for additional responsibilities at school, (5) respect and friendship from other students at school, (6) excellent letters of recommendation from teachers when applying to college, (7) admission into a good college or university, (8) the possibility of a scholarship, (9) the completion of college credits before even entering college, (10) opportunities to go to an excellent college overseas for additional study, (11) the prospect of getting a good job or internship while attending college, (12) the opportunity to attend an excellent graduate school, if desired, and (13) the likelihood of getting a good job after graduating from college.

I am sure that parents and students have heard or thought about many of these benefits of making good grades, but I will develop each of them in detail to underscore their importance. I will also show parents how to make arguments that will create respect for education so their children will be motivated to do well in school. The next time students ask, "Why should I work my rear end off in school?" parents will have a ready answer.

A Feeling of Confidence and Self-Esteem

A feeling of confidence and self-esteem is one of the most important ingredients for success not only in school but in life, and making good grades is certainly a good way to attain these attributes. After all, what good grades say is that a student has performed in an exemplary manner on a set of academic courses for the term or semester. Whether in school, sports, or life in general, people who have been successful in the past are more likely to succeed in the future because they have confidence that they will succeed. Excellence breeds excellence, and those who think they will succeed end up succeeding—it is a self-fulfilling prophecy. This should come as no surprise because one's state of mind, one's confidence and self-esteem, directly influences one's performance. I do not know whether this trait comes from the fact that confident people are sure of their abilities and do not falter in their actions, or from setting high standards and not settling for anything less, but the phenomenon is real.

An academic transcript becomes a track record of what a student has done in the past, and reflects what the student and others expect the level of performance to be in the future. When students who have made good grades in the past are confronted with a difficult new subject, they do not shy away from the challenge because they are confident that they can overcome it, as they have done with other difficult subjects in the past.

Satisfaction for a Job Well Done

Whatever a person's vocation or avocation, there is pride in accomplishment and satisfaction for a job well done. The same feelings apply to students. When a student has received a good grade on a test or a paper, there is an initial feeling of satisfaction for getting over a hurdle in a successful manner. If the teacher has written complimentary remarks on the test or paper, as they often do, describing the specific nature of the accomplishment, then this enhances the feeling because someone else has recognized the effort. The situation is really no different for a master craftsman. When a skilled woodworker produces an object of beauty, he or she has the satisfaction of knowing that the creation is excellent, and if a customer buying the object offers praise and admiration, then this is again recognition for a job well done.

People who have such feelings, whether students or craftsmen, develop a state of inner happiness that extends far beyond their immediate contributions and influences their overall state of well-being. People usually like to do things they are good at, and they are happier if they feel that they are making a meaningful contribution. When a student has a record of making good grades through the breadth and depth of the curriculum, this indicates excellence not only as a specialist but as a generalist. Someone who takes pride in his or her work will not settle for less than his or her best, because that person's own standards are set very high.

Less Stress at Home with Parents

There is often an intense level of stress in the home if a student is not living up to expectations. Some parents put the bar for academic success much higher for their children than do others, but I assure you that all parents are dissatisfied if a child brings home mediocre or failing grades. The lives of both parents and students can be severely impacted by such conflicts. If a parent is unhappy enough, there may be a scolding, extensive verbal derision, and the removal of privileges. Hours can be consumed by such conflicts, time that could have been spent studying, and both parents and students withdraw from the exchange with an intense level of dissatisfaction. The student may go off sulking, wasting more hours that could have been spent studying. Parents are consumed by such miseries and often carry them off to work, because they care so much about their children's success.

The best policy is for students to do what is expected in school, which will be reflected in the grades they receive. Parents and their children should have a long talk with each other, in which the parents clearly lay out their expectations and describe what will happen if the children meet or do not meet these expectations.

An Opportunity for Additional Responsibilities at School

A student who has demonstrated his or her capability by making good grades will likely have the opportunity for additional responsibilities at school. School administrators and teachers regard good students as reliable citizens who are responsible and trustworthy. They may enlist these students to help or tutor other students who are struggling with their studies. Educators sometimes believe that students can communicate information to a peer even more effectively than can teachers, because students often have similar ways of thinking about things. If a student has shown an ability to tutor and is willing to spend extra time in the task, teachers will often give such a student other opportunities, such as helping out when setting up and running a lab in a science course. Such activities look very impressive when they are listed on an application for college.

Teachers also tend to recruit good students to participate in a variety of extracurricular activities, such as science clubs, mathematics clubs, photography clubs, and a number of other activities that take place in the school environment. Because these clubs are normally run by a teacher who has an interest in a particular subject or area, they provide an important venue for students to get to know their teachers better in a more casual setting, as well as getting to know other students with similar interests. All of these activities look impressive on a college application, and they can make an important difference, especially when a student is applying to a competitive school or falls short in some other areas. Although assuming such responsibilities takes a fair amount of time, and there is a real danger in trying to do too much, students should assume as much additional responsibility in school as is feasible.

Respect and Friendship from Other Students at School

Surveys have shown that good students are more popular with their peers than are poor students, especially as students age and become more mature. Although some groups of students tease or make fun of good students, this is the exception rather than the rule. Other students in a class are often impressed with the accomplishments of the star students, especially in a difficult subject. In addition, other students learn more from having good students in their class, because good students typically ask good questions, which raises the classroom discussion to a higher level. Good students also serve as effective role models, as other students try to emulate their behavior. As noted by nineteenth-century English author Charles Caleb Colton, "Imitation is the sincerest form of flattery." Because most students look up to good students for their abilities, good students will have an advantage over weaker students when running for class offices, such as president or vice president of the student body.

Students should be encouraged to make good grades, not only because they will have more friends, but because they will have more of the right kind of friends. Make no mistake—peer groups are very important for shaping behavior, particularly in younger, more impressionable minds. If students have friends who put a high premium on doing well in school, then they are likely to adopt similar behavior.

Excellent Letters of Recommendation from Teachers when Applying to College

A big advantage that good students have over poor students is being able to obtain impressive letters of recommendation from their teachers when applying to college. If you have kept up with stories in the news, then you know that it is becoming increasingly more difficult for students to be accepted into competitive colleges. That is because good colleges are being inundated by a number of applications from students who have good grades, many extracurricular activities, and high scores on standardized tests such as the SAT. Many good students will be turned away, and usually the deciding difference was that other students looked slightly better qualified. In this regard, a student will have an important advantage if he or she can obtain impressive letters of recommendation from teachers. Most teachers are very discerning about writing letters of recommendation because they do not want to give exaggerated impressions that could question their future credibility if a student does not live up to expectations. On the other hand, if someone has been an especially good student and worked very hard, most teachers feel that they owe him or her something in return.

The advantage of a good letter of recommendation is that it goes beyond quantitative information like a GPA or a score on a standardized test, and provides qualitative information on the student as a person. For example, if a teacher says that a student is absolutely brilliant, works extremely hard, helps other students in class, raises the level of discussion in the classroom, and has tremendous potential for future success, this is bound to make a favorable impression on a college admissions officer. It is important to develop rapport with teachers of subjects in which the student has a keen interest and has done well. Make sure not to wait too long before asking for a letter of recommendation.

Admission into a Good College or University

I am not overstating the case when I say that a student's grades are the single most important factor in determining what kind of college will accept him or her for admission. College curriculums can be very difficult, particularly at competitive schools, and universities want to make sure that they are making a good investment when accepting one student and denying another. It is essential to their institutional reputation and their future revenue stream. The reason good grades are so important is that they indicate not only what a student is capable of doing but also what that student has done in the past. If you were a college admissions officer, and you saw on a transcript that a student had a track record of making nearly all A's semester after semester, and year after year, especially in difficult courses, wouldn't you have greater confidence that the student was likely to do the same once in your college?

Although colleges have many dimensions, at the core their most important function is imparting and extending knowledge, and that is why good grades relate directly to their core competency. Good colleges want the type of students who will add to their reputation as an excellent institution of learning. Parents should encourage their children to put forth their best effort all through high school (and junior high school) to make the highest grades possible to get into the best college possible. Not only will this enrich their educational experience, there is evidence that it will help them later on, because students who graduate from good schools are more likely to have better jobs and higher incomes than are students who graduate from weaker schools.

The Possibility of a Scholarship

Students who make good grades in school are much more likely to get an academic scholarship to college than students who make poor grades. Colleges offer academic scholarships to students with good grades because they want to attract superior students who will enhance the college's reputation and raise the level of classroom performance. Even students who are candidates to get a scholarship based on their athletic prowess are more likely to get the scholarship if they also have good grades, because schools do not want to give scholarships to students who cannot make the grade in college, which will bar them from playing their sport.

The value of a college scholarship can be substantial.

The cost of going to college has increased very rapidly in recent times, creating a financial burden on families that pay for their children's education or students who take out a loan to finance their education. Scholarships often cover all or part of the cost of tuition, the cost of books, and sometimes in graduate school a stipend as well, particularly if the student is supplying a service such as being a teaching or research assistant. My son, Chris, who was an excellent student all through school, received offers of scholarships at both the undergraduate and graduate levels. If parents want their children to be eligible for a scholarship, they should start working on this goal from the earliest possible grades, and make sure that the students receive good grades all through school.

Completion of College Credits Before Even Entering College

The four major routes to obtain college credits before entering college are through Advanced Placement (AP) courses, the College-Level Examination Program (CLEP), the International Baccalaureate (IB) program, and Cambridge International Examinations (CIE). See "Educational Resources" (appendix C) at the back of the book for links to descriptions of each program. Advanced Placement courses are the most widespread and widely accepted, so I will concentrate my remarks in this section on them.

Students who make good grades in high school are much more likely to be accepted into Advanced Placement courses, which will enable them to complete a number of college credits even before entering college. Competition to get into Advanced Placement courses is very rigorous because only a limited number of teachers teach the courses, resulting in a limited number of slots for students. Only the best students will be accepted into these courses because the material is much more difficult than the typical high school course, and the workload is much heavier because the student receives full college credit for the course. A student who plans to major in mathematics or the physical sciences in college should take a full complement of Advanced Placement courses in mathematics, biology, chemistry, and physics. A student who plans to major in the social sciences should take a full complement of Advanced Placement courses in English, history, and government.

Regardless of a student's planned major, it is a good idea to take Advanced Placement courses in as many of the subjects I have listed as possible. Not only will the student enter college with a substantial number of credits completed, it will be easier to get into the college of his or her choice because of taking these courses. Moreover, students who take Advanced Placement courses in high school will find subjects easier once in college because they have already encountered the more difficult material.

It is also a good idea for students to take a foreign language for four years in high school so none will be required in college, unless they want to major in a foreign language. My son, Chris, took Advanced Placement courses and foreign language courses all through high school, and benefited greatly from the experience. Not having to take foreign language courses in college enables students to take more courses in their major or additional electives.

It is never too soon for students to begin thinking about taking Advanced Placement courses. At the earliest possible convenience, students should meet with their guidance counselor to discuss courses offered in the Advanced Placement program, which courses need to be taken to qualify for them, the order in which they should be taken, and how they will impact the students' academic workload. Students who wait too long to have these discussions may find that they have not had adequate preparation or that all of the available slots have already been taken.

Opportunities to Go to an Excellent College Overseas for Additional Study

A student who makes good grades in high school and college will have increased opportunities to attend an excellent college overseas for additional study. The United States has some of the finest colleges and universities in the world, and many foreign students come to our country for study, but that should not preclude looking at opportunities elsewhere. Attending college is one of the most broadening experiences possible in a person's life because there is an opportunity to live in a new location, meet new people, and learn new things. The experience can be broadened even further by attending a top college overseas, if only for a semester or the summer, particularly if it is a world-renowned university and has faculty that possess unique knowledge about a subject not available from domestic sources. Not only is this a wonderful experience for the student, it looks very attractive on the résumé, particularly if a student will later be applying to graduate school.

The world is becoming an increasingly smaller place in terms of international interaction, and overseas study affords the opportunity to make contacts at both the student and faculty level that will be valuable for a lifetime. Sometimes a student will hear about such offers by making good grades, because top foreign schools typically are interested only in the best students. While an undergraduate at George Mason University in Virginia, my daughter Dana received several offers to apply for independent study at Oxford University in England.

If an unsolicited offer for international study does not

appear automatically in the mail, there are several things students can do to learn about such opportunities through their school. In high school, announcements can often be found through guidance and foreign language departments. In college, opportunities for foreign study may be found in a number of locations, including the student union, international studies departments, foreign language departments, and also through a number of different departments that one does not normally associate with foreign study. Most departments post announcements about such opportunities on a central bulletin board or online message board. Both high school and college programs typically include opportunities for summer study as well as during the regular school year. Whether one is in high school or college, it is important to talk to a knowledgeable person at the school who can provide important information about the extent of the commitment, the nature of the curriculum, whether the courses are taught in English, how much it will cost, whether the courses will count for credit, and whether the experience will have an impact on the time of graduation.

Opportunities for foreign study are handled through many different organizations. There are a number of exchange student organizations, such as the American Field Service, the Rotary Youth Exchange, and the Youth for Understanding Foundation, to name a few. The Council for Standards on International Educational Travel maintains a list of vetted programs throughout America. The American Institute for Foreign Study facilitates a number of foreign college study programs in countries around the world. Arrangements for foreign study at the collegiate level are often quite varied, and may include funding from governments, private foundations, and reciprocal arrangements among departments in domestic and international colleges and universities. Students who are interested in foreign study should begin their research early, both to learn about the most suitable programs and to take advantage of available openings. "Educational Resources" (appendix C) at the back of this book contains online links to the organizations I have mentioned.

The Prospect of Getting a Good Job or Internship While Attending College

A very significant advantage of making good grades in school is the opportunity to get a job or internship when school is not in session. Few students attend college year round full-time, so it is wise both intellectually and financially to be doing other meaningful things during the summer or even part-time when school is in session. Companies and organizations will make offers for part-time employment and internships to only the best students, so students interested in such opportunities have a strong incentive to earn a high grade-point average. The advantage of working for a company before graduating from college is that a student gets to see what the working world is like, while making money to finance a college education, and the company gets to take a close look at a potential new employee in the actual work environment. Many students have benefited from such arrangements, and find that they have a job offer waiting as soon as they graduate from college, particularly if they put forth their best effort while working as a student. Working at an early age also has the advantage of producing a mature outlook, with strong incentives to do even better in school because a real, tangible goal can be seen on the horizon.

If a student is serious about attending graduate school, one of the best activities possible is to get an internship at a top think tank, such as the American Enterprise Institute for Public Policy Research, where I worked. Although typically an intern is not paid for his or her work, colleges often give credit for completing an internship. Having such valuable experience on a résumé can help open the doors to some of the top graduate and professional schools in the world. Because of the fierce competition for such opportunities, it is recommended that students start looking early.

Students interested in internships can do several things to prepare for the experience. The first task is to decide on an appropriate organization, one that does work in an area that students are interested in and that provides an opportunity to get involved in important projects with well-known colleagues. For example, students interested in working at top think tanks can easily visit their Web sites to learn about the type of work such organizations do and who is employed there. To gain entry, they will need to build a strong résumé that highlights their education, achievements, and aspirations. Students who need advice on how to create a résumé can easily get guidance from any number of books available in the library or even online. Although résumés sent without solicitation to a top organization may get some consideration, a far better approach is for students to meet someone within the organization who can make a recommendation. This may seem difficult if students do not know anyone within the organization, but sometimes a well-stated e-mail with an interesting question will pique the interest of an important person, opening up the opportunity for additional communication or even a personal visit.

The Opportunity to Attend an Excellent Graduate School

Good grades are essential to get into a top school not only as an undergraduate student, but also as a graduate student. There was a time, many decades ago, when it was sufficient for someone to have a high school degree to obtain a good job. Then, as time passed, the bar was raised and the good jobs went to people with a college degree at the undergraduate level. In today's world, having an undergraduate degree in many fields is not sufficient to get a top job, and advanced training at the master's or even the doctorate level is required. And, of course, many professional fields such as medicine and law require not only professional training but also certification. More and more people, men and women alike, are attending graduate school these days, and to be admitted to a top graduate school an applicant needs excellent grades as an undergraduate, and most likely a good score on the Graduate Record Examination (GRE) as well.

Students who plan to take the GRE, or for that matter, any standardized test for admission to a college or university, should take some preliminary steps to prepare in advance. Any number of practice questions for standardized tests are available for free online. Alternatively, books with practice questions for standardized tests are available from the library or bookstores. By working through these practice questions ahead of time, students will understand the nature and format of the questions and be better prepared when taking the actual test. Students who want more formal instruction on taking standardized tests can enroll in courses offered by organizations that specialize in preparing students for such tests. The advantage of taking a course is that students have the opportunity to interact with a knowledgeable expert who can diagnose problems they are having and offer strategies for overcoming them. Organizations that offer courses to prepare students for taking standardized tests are well advertised on the Internet. Such organizations charge a fee for their services, but the expense may be worthwhile if the personal instruction helps students to pass a critical examination.

Some students start out as an undergraduate knowing that they eventually want to attend graduate or professional school, and others arrive at this decision only after several years as an undergraduate. The important point is that students who have obtained good grades through the undergraduate years will have the option of attending graduate school, and also attending one of high caliber. I am sure that you have heard the familiar advice of always keeping your options open, and making good grades is one of the best ways to do this.

The Likelihood of Getting a Good Job upon Graduation from College

For those who want to go directly into the world of work after graduating from college, good grades are one of the best ways possible of getting that desirable job that everyone else graduating wants. I will not say too much about the subject here because the next chapter deals exclusively with how a good education will get you a good job. However, it is important to emphasize that employers put high value on a student's getting good grades for three reasons: (1) good grades indicate that the student is smart enough to master complex material, (2) good grades indicate that the student is conscientious and willing to follow instructions and do work, and (3) good grades indicate that the student is trainable. All three skills are essential to be successful in the working world. I know that when I worked as a supervisor during my approximately forty years of work experience, I always put a high premium on students' having good grades before I would hire them. And although my intuitions were not always correct every time, they were correct most of the time, which kept me following the same practice.

Parents should encourage their children to work hard in school and get good grades so they will not have to work in a boring and low-paying job. Plenty of low-grade jobs are available in our economy for people who do not have any education. What these jobs have in common is low pay, hard work, and unpleasant working conditions, usually without any amenities such as employer-provided health insurance. It is most likely that students who goof off in school will be working in these jobs for the rest of their lives without any hope of advancement, and they will have to be satisfied with their situation because they will not have any alternatives. Although there is dignity in all types of work, why settle for something less than your potential, especially when you are young and can do something about it?

Comparing School to Work

An approach that has always worked for me as a parent when emphasizing the importance of good grades is to compare school with work. Whatever their line of work, parents undoubtedly get up every day to go to work and put forth a strong effort, either because they take great pride in their work or because they do not want to be fired. They do these things because it is their job, and a job demands a certain level of responsibility. Parents can communicate the same feeling to their children by describing school as being their job. The analogy is straightforward: They have to get up early, get dressed, arrive on time, do assignments, and be evaluated on their work.

Parents should explain to their children that although they do not get paid in money for their efforts in school, in a sense they do get paid by receiving a good grade that will enable them to continue on at a higher level of study, which will eventually lead to a higher level of work that will bring a higher level of pay. The only difference is that the monetary part of the reward is delayed. Just as parents show the proper attitude toward work, students should show the proper attitude toward school. The entire world works because people do their job at the proper level, and if they did not, then everything would rapidly start to break down.

As with work, good students put forth their greatest effort in school so they will be proud of their accomplishments.

Parents can choose as an analogy some task they performed on their own job in which they demonstrated their skill or were recognized for their accomplishments. They can describe that special inner feeling that comes from knowing that they did something extremely well, something they were very proud of. If these efforts helped others to accomplish their tasks more effectively, or if they were recognized by a supervisor or peers, this should be mentioned as well. These inner feelings and feedback from others are what give us not only immediate gratification, but also the motivation to perform at an even higher level in the future. Parents should explain to their children that the situation in school is no different: They will feel good about doing exemplary work on an assignment or test, which will likely be recognized by the teacher and other peers.

If parents need to provide additional explanation, here is a more direct way to describe the situation: If students have to be at school anyway, just as parents have to be at work, then why not put forth the best effort to get the most recognition, rather than just going through the motions?

Creating the Right Atmosphere

One of the most important things parents can do to establish the value of making good grades is to instill in their children the proper level of respect and importance about education. Did you know that in Japan teaching, at any level, is considered to be one of the most honorable professions in society? Not only do teachers command more respect and reverence than in the United States, they are paid accordingly. This is how it should be because teachers have the duty of developing knowledgeable, effective, and responsible citizens that will determine the future success of a nation.

Parents should talk to their children about the important function of education and the essential role that teachers play in our society. They can relate stories of the memorable teachers in their own background—we all have had them!—and emphasize how those educators influenced their life in some significant way. In fact, talking is not enough! Parents should demonstrate their respect by meeting their children's teachers through PTA meetings or other school events, learning about their backgrounds and expertise, and communicating their impressions and feelings to their children. Parents should never downgrade the importance of the school administrators, the curriculum, or particular teachers they may not like or think highly of, because how can students be expected to show the proper level of respect if parents do not? If students develop the proper level of respect about their school and its officials, vigorous work effort and good grades will follow naturally.

It also does not hurt if parents tell their children how important success in school is to them personally. Parents should be very open about the fact that they think continuously about the success of their children in school because they know how important it will be for their success in life. Children are a projection of their parents' desires, and parents naturally want their children to succeed for their own happiness, continuation of the bloodline and, perhaps subconsciously, for perpetuation of the species. If parents worry about the performance of their children in school, particularly when they are doing poorly, they should not be hesitant to reflect these feelings as well.

Most students want to do the things that their parents desire, even though they are occasionally rebellious, and they want their parents to recognize their efforts. When parents show that they are interested and concerned, they help to establish a level of rapport that will give their children the feedback they need, and possibly serve as an early detection system when things go awry. For some students, the appreciation expressed for a job well done in school is just as important to them as the grade that appears on their report card. Remember, first and foremost, parents are their children's most important teacher, so it is important for them to guide their progress and provide approbation.

RECAP

Getting good grades:

1. Builds confidence and self-esteem
2. Creates numerous opportunities
3. Increases the likelihood of getting into a good college or graduate school
4. Increases the likelihood of getting a good job upon graduation

---

5

How to Engage in Effective Job Planning

(So students will be motivated to work hard in school)

Seventeenth-century Japanese poet Ihara Saikaku said, "The first consideration for all, throughout life, is the earning of a living." The way most of us make our living is through our occupation, and the occupation we practice is very much a function of the education we possess.

Unfortunately, the basic relationship between education and occupation seems to escape the understanding of many young students. Parents ask their children when they are very young, "What do you want to be when you grow up?" Common answers they may hear are "a doctor," "a lawyer," or "an airplane pilot," because youngsters tend to associate these professions with excitement as well as success, both financially and socially. All three of those occupations require a tremendous investment in education, because without education there is no way to enter them, as is true of many other desirable occupations. However, many students fail to understand that the time they spend in school, and how well they do in their studies, are important first steps toward making their dreams come true. One of the most important things parents can do is to help their children think about the occupation that they want to enter and to establish the relationship between education and that occupation. When students understand this relationship, they will be more motivated to do well in school because they will know what they are working for.

Knowing what occupation one wants to pursue is not an easy task, at any age. Some years back, when a good friend of mine retired from the federal government, I asked him, "What do you plan to do now?" His response was "I still do not know what I want to do when I grow up!" Obviously, he was attempting to be humorous, but the sad truth is that many if not most people do not know what they want to do for a living until they are much older, and some never do find out.

It is very difficult to become motivated to study very hard and do one's best in school when one does not know what one is doing it for, regardless of the exhortations from parents and mentors. It is also true that many people think they know what they want to do for a living, but they often change their minds several times before making a final decision. This is okay, because often we do not know what a job entails until we start to prepare for it or actually practice it, and it would be unwise to spend the rest of our lives at a job we do not really enjoy. However, as I learned when writing an earlier book, *Getting Ahead at Work,* some of the most successful people knew at a very early age exactly what they wanted to do for a living and this provided them not only with motivation, but a lifetime to prepare and work toward making their dreams come true. That is why parents cannot begin too soon in getting their children to think about an occupation, and to understand the connection between school and work.

In this chapter, I will give you several pointers to start thinking about a future occupation and what will be needed to enter it. One of the most important reasons for obtaining additional education is to be able to enter a certain occupation. Because the desire to enter a particular occupation is therefore one of the strongest inducements to do well in school, I will devote considerable attention to this matter, including some exercises to stimulate thought.

The Importance of an Occupation

To start, in our society education is the key that opens all doors. We are so fortunate not to live in a caste society, which is still present in many parts of the world, in which people are obligated to pursue the education and profession of their parents and are not given any alternatives. I would wager that many of these people would be overjoyed if they could take the place of an American student, even with all of the work, and have a chance to prepare for what they really want to do with their lives. What many people in our society, especially children, fail to realize is that you literally can become anything you want in our society if you are prepared to undertake the effort for meeting the requirements for admission.

If a student wants to become a doctor, he or she needs to know that it will be important to do well all through school, major in disciplines that are scientific, spend long hours in laboratories as an undergraduate in college, and spend even longer hours in medical school, followed by a taxing period of internship—but becoming a doctor is achievable if one is committed. I will not deny that the task will be more difficult for people who are not wealthy, given the high cost of medical school, but the goal can be achieved regardless of one's background if the desire is present. Pick any other professional occupation and you will find that the path is also very arduous.

In talking to students, parents should emphasize that choosing an occupation is one of the most important decisions a person ever makes. The occupation we pursue determines how we spend most of our time and how we think about our lives. The time we spend at work consumes a significant part of our daily lives, and most of us spend more time at work than we spend at home with our family or friends. What we do for a living often influences our friendships, because we meet individuals pursuing similar endeavors who have similar interests. An occupation becomes part of our self-identity, and influences our feelings about self-worth and achievement. When we meet someone new, one of the first things he or she asks is, "What do you do for a living?" And when we answer, we create an impression about our relative position and importance in society, and what we have to contribute.

An occupation directly affects our level of happiness and financial well-being. People who love their job look forward to going to work every day, and people who despise their job (and there are plenty!) dread the thought of getting up in the morning. Most important, the salaries we receive from our job provide the means for making a living and make possible a number of other things that we want to achieve. Choosing an occupation is central to future success and happiness, and education is the key that makes all things possible.

Introspective Exercises

Parents, teachers, relatives, and friends often encourage students to pursue occupations that require great intellect, use special skills, and pay vast sums of money. Although such advice often motivates some students in a particular direction, it can result in dissatisfaction and failure for others. The wise approach is not to accept someone else's definition of success for an occupation, but to look inward to decide what one really wants.

A student thinking about a future occupation should ask, "What activity would I like to be doing, even if I were not paid for it?" The key here is our mental assessment that when we do something for ourselves we call it "play," and when we do it for others we call it "work." Earlier I used the analogy of a child playing in a sandbox. You do not have to pay children to play in a sandbox, because they love it so much they will do it for free. People who really love their work are like children at play in the sandbox, totally preoccupied with what they are doing and exploring the various ramifications of their work, while trying to achieve a result that approximates their idea of perfection. People are much happier when they are doing something at work that brings meaning and enjoyment to their lives, rather than just showing up to make a living.

The situation is very different for people who hate their work. They view their job as necessary drudgery to earn a living, and each minute at work seems like another step on an endless treadmill. They end up watching the clock, waiting for each day to end and for the workweek to be over so they can begin their real lives. If students are unhappy with school, parents should get them to think about all of the people who are unhappy with their job. We are not talking about an experience that ends after a few years but goes on for the rest of one's life, with no summer break!

It is difficult for a student to think about an occupation if he or she has never worked, or worked only sporadically, so it is important to point out that although people are different, they all have basic fundamental needs. For example, we all have physiological needs for food, clothing, housing, and other necessities, and we all need a safe and secure place where these needs will be met in the future. We also have a need to interact with others in a social context and be accepted by the group, and to excel and achieve status from some activity. Self-fulfillment comes from using our skills and abilities in a creative manner. Therefore, it should be easy to see that an occupation helps us meet these various needs, from the most basic to the more complex. That is why it is so important to obtain a good education that will enable the student to enter the occupation of his or her choice.

Parents should point out that although everyone agrees about basic attributes of a job that are desirable, they are likely to disagree about activities that are desirable. For example, everyone would agree that a desirable job has pleasant working conditions, tasks that are stimulating and rewarding, and a large salary. However, as Carl Jung, the famous Swiss psychiatrist, noted, there are four different functions that people use to receive and process information: thinking, intuiting, feeling, and sensing. All people possess and use some combination of these functions in their everyday lives and at work, but they tend to excel in a particular direction. For example, thinkers tend to excel in occupations that require analysis of facts and figures; intuitors tend to do best in occupations that allow them to use their imagination to plan and create; feelers tend to excel in occupations that involve extensive personal contact; and sensors tend to have an advantage in occupations involving implementing, negotiating, and troubleshooting. One's innate abilities along these various dimensions usually arise very early, so students should think deeply about the function or activity in which they tend to excel. A good strategy is to identify an occupation that will regularly require the use of this function, and then work steadily to obtain the education needed to enter it.

In ancient Greece, the following advice, often attributed to the Seven Sages, was inscribed on the temple of Apollo at Delphi: "Know thyself." There is probably no better advice when thinking about an occupation in which one will be happy and successful. We all have a unique set of skills, abilities, and preferences, and when these are combined in the proper manner in a job, the stage is set for each of us to excel.

Activities that Yielded Exceptional Satisfaction and Accomplishment

To help students identify this unique set of skills, abilities, and preferences, they are encouraged to think about previous activities, whether at work or otherwise, that yielded exceptional satisfaction and accomplishment. It is very likely that the activities that brought such satisfaction and accomplishment in the past will also do so in the future, when practiced in a particular occupation. The goal is to match one's skills, abilities, and preferences to the requirements of a job, because this will bring both happiness and success. To help students do this, I suggest that they think introspectively about three areas: (1) previous summer jobs, (2) major accomplishments, (3) and innermost dreams.

Summer Jobs

Summer jobs provide wonderful opportunities for students to have a productive summer and earn money to save for college, or even spend on frivolous activities if they so desire. They also provide a unique opportunity for students to learn about different lines of work, and to find out specifically what they like and do not like about particular jobs. Students should think back about all previous summer jobs they held.

It is important to think about the description of the job, the duties and responsibilities involved, the knowledge and skills required, and whether the job involved working primarily with data, people, or things. Students should then make an honest assessment of how well they performed in various aspects of the job, and what they particularly liked or did not like about the job. In most cases, the two factors will be closely correlated.

Students should then think about a particular skill and set of environmental conditions that predominated in the various summer jobs that they liked, and whether it involved working with data, people, or things. For example, if students held both physical and sedentary summer jobs, did they prefer manual dexterity or mental capability at work? Did they prefer a laid-back environment with routine work, or a challenging environment with opportunities for innovation? Did they prefer a safe and secure job with a predictable rate of pay, or one that entailed risks with large potential payoffs (which usually means large potential penalties, as well!)? Were they able to tell from a summer job whether they liked extensive interaction with other people, or preferred to work in a solitary environment? Did they have an opportunity to work in a company with a variety of different environmental factors—such as companies of different size, the experience of indoor and outdoor work, and different work hours, dress codes, and travel requirements?

All of these experiences help people to identify their own unique set of skills, abilities, and preferences, so they can think more clearly about the type of job they would like to be doing for the rest of their lives. Now I think you can see the value of summer jobs in helping to determine one's future profession. And, as I noted earlier, when students know what they want to do for a living, they will be much more strongly motivated to obtain the education needed to make their dreams come true!

Major Accomplishments

One's major accomplishments in life, even at a very early age, also provide valuable information about the choice of a future occupation. Students should think about their major accomplishments, whether they involved achievements in school, activities in their summer jobs, or activities they undertook purely for leisure. For example, an accomplishment might involve a subject that the student particularly liked in school and excelled at. It might involve some particular activity in a summer job in which the supervisor or a customer noted that the student had an exceptional skill, which resulted in much satisfaction and pride. Or it might involve a host of other activities, such as hobbies, sports, voluntary or community activities, family life, special projects, or any other activity that was noteworthy and provided enjoyment. Even though a student may be very young, it is wise to think back over his or her entire lifetime when identifying these activities. Sometimes people have a unique skill, ability, or preference that will appear early in the most unlikely of locations.

The next task is to review these major accomplishments in terms of the skills, abilities, and knowledge that were required to carry them out successfully. Students should think about whether the accomplishments involved data, people, or things, and what they did best or liked the most about each of the accomplishments. It is important to identify the skills, abilities, and knowledge that recur most often, because these are likely to be the ones that will bring the most success and satisfaction in a job. The goal is to identify an occupation that requires the same set of skills, abilities, and knowledge, so that one can pursue it to make a living. When people are very satisfied and proficient in their work, the financial rewards tend to follow naturally. If students have been very diligent in pursuing this activity, then they should now know what they are looking for in a job. In the next exercise, students should look deeply inward and think about their innermost dreams.

Innermost Dreams

We all have innermost dreams about what we really want out of life, whether they involve fame, power, knowledge, accomplishment, wealth, physical prowess, beauty, love, friendship, truth, integrity, or freedom—*or perhaps all of them*! It makes perfect sense to look for a job that enables us to realize our innermost dreams. Students should think about an ideal job that embodies as many of these desirable characteristics as possible. This ideal job should have all the right trappings for the student, and allow him or her to grow and develop in a career over time, without stress or unhappiness. It is best if this exercise proceeds without any constraints, without the worry of money, when the job will be available, or the qualifications needed to perform it. The student should think as broadly as possible, and not worry about whether the dream is realistic. It does not hurt to shoot for the moon, especially when one is young and all things are possible. When a person wants something badly enough, this is often the first step in making it become a reality.

Now, let me offer some advice that will enable students' dreams about their ideal jobs to be more focused and realistic. Students should think about the activities and functions that they would really enjoy doing in a job. The dream will be more structured if students think about whether they want to work with facts and figures, produce tangible products, or be of service to other people. The types of goods produced and services provided should be consistent with their own set of values. Next, students should think about ideal surroundings at work. Do they want to work in a large or small company, and in what type of industry? How about the immediate surroundings, such as the size and location of the office, or the number and type of people they will be working with, and in what role? Do they want to make noteworthy contributions, or be in a power position to supervise other people? The answers to these questions should help students to come up with a tangible idea of their ideal job.

There is one more piece of advice that is essential when thinking about one's ideal job, and it is the following: There is a definite correlation between the skill required to do a job and job satisfaction. It is almost an axiom that people will enjoy a job and be proficient in it if the job requires skills that they are very adept at and enjoy using. Students may have studied a subject in school that indicates a strong aptitude, but if they do not enjoy studying the subject, then it is unlikely that they would enjoy working in a field that requires the same knowledge. Whether in school or at work, both conditions are essential for a good match: skill and enjoyment. If you have ever worked in a job that fell short of your ideal choice, then you know that it is difficult to maintain your proficiency and production over the long run, especially if your heart is not in it. The goal is to find a vocation that involves both skill and enjoyment, because then it will seem like an avocation.

Occupational Outlook Handbook

If students have gone through these various exercises faithfully, they should have a good idea of an ideal job that embodies all of the desirable elements. Even if students did not come up with a specific job, the odds are that they now know a lot more about what they are looking for in a job. Now is the time for students to learn much more about the specific characteristics of the chosen occupation, or to identify a job that has the desired characteristics. I am going to introduce you to a resource called the *Occupational Outlook Handbook,* which is published by the U.S. Bureau of Labor Statistics. The handbook is one of the most useful publications issued by the federal government, and is available in libraries and, more conveniently, online (www.bls.gov/oco/) at no charge. It contains detailed information about most of the major occupations in our economy.

The *Occupational Outlook Handbook* is very useful to a student thinking about a future occupation because it describes just about everything one would want to know about an occupation, organized into nine easy-to-follow sections. I am going to review each of these sections in detail because this is such a valuable resource for people thinking about entering an occupation, and then I will provide an example for one specific occupation: lawyers.

Section 1: *Nature of the work.* This section describes the typical duties workers perform in their job, the type of equipment and tools they use, the nature and closeness of supervision provided, and how they interact with other workers in the workplace. It also describes the work environment, such as the normal workweek, including the usual number of hours worked per week, typical work schedules, and whether overtime work is available or required. Also included are physical and psychological demands of the job, and whether the work is indoors or outdoors, clean or dirty, quiet or noisy, safe or hazardous, and so forth.

Section 2: *Training, other qualifications, and advancement.* This section describes the level of formal education, training, and other qualifications that determine whether someone can enter an occupation and how rapidly he or she is likely to advance. (This section is particularly important to students because it describes how much education they will need to enter the occupation.)

Section 3: *Employment*. This section describes the number of jobs in the occupation, and whether the jobs are concentrated in the private, public, or nonprofit sector; in particular industries or geographical areas; and the incidence of self-employment and part-time work.

Section 4: *Job outlook*. This section contains a discussion of the expected change in available jobs in the occupation for the next ten years, the types of positions and duties that will be available, and whether the jobs will be located in the private, public, or nonprofit sectors.

Section 5: *Projections data*. This section contains a tabular presentation showing projections of the expected number of jobs in the occupation over the next decade, including both the number of jobs that will be created and the percentage change.

Section 6: *Earnings*. This section describes the median (average) annual earnings for all persons in the occupation, the salary range for the middle half of the distribution, how these earnings vary across industries, and supplementary information on entry level earnings. (This section is particularly important to students because the level of earnings in an occupation is often a strong incentive to do well in school to gain entry.)

Section 7: *Related occupations*. This section describes other related occupations that require similar education, aptitudes, interests, skills, and abilities as the occupation in question.

Section 8: *Sources of additional information*. This section contains a variety of useful contact information, such as the names and addresses of various organizations that supply pertinent information about the occupation or administer certification to enter the occupation, as well as career and counseling information for special groups, such as the handicapped.

Section 9: *OOH O*NET codes.* This section contains a set of numbers from the *Occupational Outlook Handbook* (OOH) Occupational Information Network (O*NET), which is a system used by state employment service offices to classify applicants and job openings. It is also used by some libraries and career information centers to file occupational information. The beauty of the O*NET system is that users can use the codes to search for occupations that match their skills, and obtain a vast amount of information about the occupation, as described in the sections above.

With this information at their fingertips, students can learn just about everything that they need to know about an occupation, and see in black and white why education is so important to enter the occupation. This information can be obtained for just about any occupation in the economy, but I will select and describe one—lawyers—to illustrate the utility of the approach. I will briefly summarize information about the occupation of lawyers for each of the nine major sections in the *Occupational Outlook Handbook:*

Section 1: *Nature of the work.* Lawyers, also called attorneys, act as advocates by representing clients in civil or criminal trials, and also act as advisers by counseling their clients on legal rights and obligations. All lawyers are licensed to represent their clients in court, but trial lawyers specialize in trial work. Lawyers concentrate in a number of different areas, such as bankruptcy, probate (wills), international, environment, and intellectual property, to name a few. Most lawyers are in private practice, but many work at several levels of government. Lawyers conduct their business in offices, law libraries, and courtrooms. They may meet with clients in their homes or places of business, and they may travel to gather evidence or appear before courts and legislative bodies. Lawyers in private practice may work long and irregular hours, conferring with clients, conducting research, or preparing briefs, especially when a case is being tried.

Section 2: *Training, other qualifications, and advancement.* The formal training for a lawyer includes four years of college, three years of law school, a requirement to pass the bar examination, and, in some states, a written ethics examination. Most law schools want students who have demonstrated proficiency in college courses that require skills in reading, speaking, writing, researching, analyzing, and thinking logically, and require them to pass the Law School Admission Test (LSAT).

Section 3: *Employment.* In 2006, there were about 761,000 jobs listed as lawyers in the United States. Most lawyers were in private practice, either as partners in law firms or in business for themselves. Most of the salaried positions for lawyers were in government, corporations, and nonprofit organizations. Among lawyers who worked for government, most were employed at the local level. Many of the salaried lawyers outside of government worked for banks, public utilities, manufacturing companies, insurance companies, and real estate firms. A relatively small number of lawyers were employed by law schools.

Section 4: *Job outlook.* Through the year 2016, employment of lawyers is expected to grow about as fast as the average for all occupations, both from the increase in population and the general level of business activity. Job openings for lawyers will increase in fields such as health care, energy, venture capital, intellectual property, antitrust, elderly issues, and environmental law. Competition for jobs will be keen because of the large number of people graduating from law school.

Section 5: *Projections data.* Between 2006 and 2016, the number of lawyers is expected to increase by 84,000 (from 761,000 to 844,000), or by about 11 percent.

Section 6: *Earnings.* In May 2006, the median (average) annual earnings of all wage-and-salaried lawyers was $102,470, and the middle half of the distribution earned between $69,910 and $145,600. Salaries of lawyers vary widely according to the size, type, and location of their employment. Salaried lawyers are likely to receive additional fringe benefits from their employer such as contributions for pension, health, and insurance plans. The median annual earnings in 2005 for lawyers who graduated from law school nine months earlier ranged from $45,000 for those who were in academic or judicial clerkships to $85,000 for those who were in private practice.

Section 7: *Related occupations.* Many other occupations require legal training, such as judges, magistrates, law clerks, paralegals and legal assistants, title examiners, searchers, abstractors, and other judicial workers.

Section 8: *Sources of additional information.* The American Bar Association is located at 321 North Clark Street, Chicago, IL 60610 (www.abanet.org). The National Association for Law Placement is located at 1025 Connecticut Avenue NW., Suite 1110, Washington, D.C. 20036 (www.nalp.org). Information on the LSAT can be found through the Law School Admission Council, P.O. Box 40, Newtown, PA 18940 (www.lsac.org).

Section 9: *OOH O*NET codes.* The OOH O*NET code for lawyers is 23-1011.00. As noted above, students can use this code to search for occupations that match their skills, and to obtain much more relevant information about the occupation of lawyers.

This brief example for the occupation of lawyers illustrates the utility of information in the *Occupational Outlook*

Handbook. Students should look up other occupations in which they are interested to find similar pertinent information, or they can just browse the handbook to learn about a variety of occupations. I suggest that they pay particular attention to section 2 on training, other qualifications, and advancement, and section 6 on earnings, because these tend to be highly motivational in encouraging a young student to study hard in order to do well in school.

Occupation and Earnings Data

I am going to close this chapter with some information from the U.S. Census Bureau that shows how earnings vary by occupation for men and women who worked year round full-time. For many years, I directed the office at the U.S. Census Bureau that produces these statistics, so I am very familiar with them and the message that they convey. I suggest that students carefully study table 2, because it really drives home the point that earnings vary significantly by occupation. The table shows mean annual earnings for several, but by no means all, of the major occupations held by men and women. I have chosen to present mean earnings, rather than median earnings, because the U.S. Census Bureau's statistical tables on occupation show a maximum value of $100,000 for median earnings, which disguises the true income level of some higher-paying occupations. Although the dollar figures will become less relevant as this edition of the book ages, I encourage you to focus on the statistics that show the ratio of mean earnings in each occupation to the overall average, because these relationships tend to remain relatively stable over time.

Table 2 provides a convenient means for ranking the various occupations by the level of earnings for men and women fifteen years old and over who worked year round full time.

Table 2. Mean Earnings in 2007 by Occupation for All Year-Round Full-Time Workers 15 Years Old and Over, by Sex.

Occupation of Longest Job	Men		Women	
	Mean Earnings	*Ratio to Total*	*Mean Earnings*	*Ratio to Total*
Total, all occupations	$58,335	1.00	$42,195	1.00
Doctors	$187,728	3.22	$102,437	2.43
Lawyers, judges, and magistrates	$168,107	2.88	$107,320	2.54
Chief executives and general managers	$136,243	2.34	$96,640	2.29
Engineers	$85,676	1.47	$65,602	1.55
Insurance sales agents	$77,570	1.33	$44,695	1.06
Postsecondary teachers	$75,601	1.30	$60,086	1.42
Computer scientists and programmers	$74,589	1.28	$68,690	1.63
Fire fighters and police	$69,043	1.18	$52,757	1.25
Nurses	$63,671	1.09	$59,507	1.41
Postal workers	$60,146	1.03	$53,342	1.26
Production workers	$41,638	0.71	$28,273	0.67
Auto, bus, taxi, and truck drivers	$41,065	0.70	$32,142	0.76
Construction workers	$40,904	0.70	$39,562	0.94
Personal care and service occupations	$39,505	0.68	$26,365	0.62
Building and grounds cleaning	$30,889	0.53	$22,894	0.54
Cashiers	$30,701	0.53	$20,563	0.49
Farming, fishing, and forestry	$26,222	0.45	$29,622	0.70
Chefs and cooks	$24,003	0.41	$23,604	0.56

Source: U.S. Census Bureau, Current Population Survey, 2008 Annual Social and Economic Supplement.

In 2007, the overall mean earnings for year-round full-time workers was $58,335 for men and $42,195 for women. The ratios in table 2 show how the earnings in a given occupation compare to the overall average. Ratios greater than 1 indicate that the occupation pays more than the overall average, and ratios less than 1 indicate that the occupation pays less than the overall average. Although women tend to earn less than men in a given occupation, for a variety of reasons, their rankings show many similarities.

One finding that stands out very clearly in table 2 is that occupations requiring higher levels of education generally pay higher earnings. The mean earnings of doctors and lawyers, both of which require very high levels of education, are roughly between two and a half to more than three times the overall mean earnings for occupations in the economy. Other occupations that require high levels of education, such as engineers, postsecondary teachers, and computer scientists and programmers, also pay more than the overall average but by a smaller degree (all of these ratios are greater than 1, but less than 2). Some occupations that do not require very high levels of education pay more than the overall average on the basis of risk, such as fire fighters and police who face physical risk, and insurance sales agents who face financial risk in terms of their earnings being dependent on commissions. At the other end of the earnings scale are occupations that do not require much education, such as production workers; auto, bus, taxi, and truck drivers; construction workers; personal care and service workers; building and grounds cleaning workers; cashiers; farming, fishing, and forestry workers; and chefs and cooks (all of these ratios are less than 1).

There is another fact that is not evident from these raw numbers on earnings, a fact noted long ago by the great American humorist Mark Twain, that is well worth remembering: "The law of work does seem utterly unfair, but there it is, and nothing can change it: the higher the pay in enjoyment the worker gets out of it, the higher shall be his pay in cash also."

Students should sit down and take a long look at the cold, hard facts of economic life ground out by the American economy, as shown in table 2. The amounts shown in the table are likely what they will be earning, on average, for the occupations they choose for the rest of their lives. Some earn more and some earn less, but the averages are indicative of what can be expected. Sure, there is a possibility that they might win the lottery, or they might make it big in professional sports, both of which would make them sinfully rich, but the odds are that they will be working in occupations such as the ones shown here for the rest of their lives. Year-round full-time work is defined as forty hours a week for fifty to fifty-two weeks a year. When people work year round full time in an occupation that does not require much education, they are probably putting in just as much effort (in their own way) as someone who works in an occupation that requires extensive education.

The relevant question for students is very clear: "Would you rather get serious with your studies now and end up in a job that will pay you handsomely and provide enjoyment for the rest of your life, or do you want to slack off with your studies now and pay the cost in terms of a less desirable occupation for the rest of your life?" *The choice is yours!*

RECAP

Students should firmly establish in their minds the strong relationship between education and occupation, which will motivate them to do well in school.

1. It is never too soon to start planning for one's future occupation.

2. All occupations are accessible if you have completed the necessary coursework and training.
3. There is significant variation in the wages of different occupations.
4. The more desirable occupations generally pay more.

2

For Students

What You Will Have to Do

6

Mastering the Basic Skills

(The right way to read a book, take a test,
and write a term paper)

English scientist and philosopher Sir Francis Bacon said, "Reading maketh a full man; conference a ready man; and writing an exact man."

These are the basic skills that you must master to become an excellent student. You must be able to read books and understand and remember what is in them; comprehend the ideas, theories, principles, and facts presented by your instructors in class; and demonstrate your mastery of all of this information in written form, in examinations, term papers, and other written assignments. If you do not possess these basic skills, you will never become a top student, no matter how hard you try. This chapter will help you master these basic skills by showing you the correct way to read books, take tests, and write term papers and other assignments.

If you have spent several years in school, you may think that you already know the correct way to read books, take

tests, and write papers. After all, as part of your assignments in school you no doubt had to read a number of books
on various different subjects, take more tests than you care
to remember, and write enough papers that would make you
an author in your own right. After all of this experience, you
probably think that you already know as much as you need to
know about reading books, taking tests, and writing papers.
However, to do something many times over does not mean
that you have learned how to do it correctly. If you are not
performing these activities in the proper manner, you may be
spending more time on your studies than is necessary, and
you may never become as good a student as you might have
become.

There is much more involved in mastering the basic
study skills than you might at first think. Hard work is truly
a virtue, and often a necessary ingredient for doing well in
school, but how you go about something is often more important than how much effort you put into it.

In this chapter, I will teach you the special techniques
that I have developed over the years for mastering the basic
skills. These techniques helped me to get an A in every course
I took while earning a Ph.D. in economics, and they have
helped countless other students excel in school while ex-
pending only the amount of effort that was absolutely necessary. I will teach you how to become an active reader so you
will understand the maximum amount from your reading assignments in the shortest amount of time. I will show you the
different strategies that will help you excel in all types of examinations, including essay exams, objective exams such as
multiple choice and true-false tests, problem exams that you
take in mathematics and science, take-home exams, open-
book exams, oral exams, and comprehensive written exams. I
will show you how to write an organized term paper that will
be a pleasure to compose and a delight to read, and I will

show you how to do it in a minimum amount of time with a minimum amount of effort.

After you master the basic skills, I will show you how to use them to become a straight-A student using the special study system I have developed. I start with reading, because it is fundamental to developing all of the other skills.

The Right Way to Read a Book
(Be an active reader, and use your unique skills to comprehend)

Saint Augustine, the legendary church father who lived during the fourth century AD, advised his students to "Take up, read! Take up, read!" His advice is just as relevant today as it was more than 1,500 years ago.

The reason books are so important is that they contain the collected wisdom of mankind, accumulated over the ages. Books constitute a permanent record of all of the scientific knowledge that has enabled us to reach our present state of technological advancement and the great literature that has helped to shape our present culture. When you read a book by a renowned author, it is almost as if you are having a conversation with and sharing the thoughts of a great thinker on a one-to-one basis. Without the permanent record provided by books, we would have to rely on word of mouth passed down from other people over generations, which would weaken the message. I hope you will develop the same reverence for books that I have, because this will make it much easier and more enjoyable for you to become a top student.

Of most importance to you, the books you read in school will help you to understand more about the subjects you are studying and to score higher on examinations. Virtually all classes from our earliest years in school have required textbooks and readings. Teachers often make reading assignments because they want their students to learn something in advance about a subject before they discuss it in class. When you already know something about a subject, it is easier to master concepts because you have already encountered them and had an opportunity to think about them. Sometimes the reading assignments will pick up where the teacher left off in class or go into far more detail than the teacher had time to present in class. The information that is contained in books often shows up later in tests, so it is essential that you have a good understanding of what is in books if you are to become a top student. Now I will show you how to get the most out of the books that you read.

Find a Comfortable Place to Read

Reading is a leisurely activity, so it is important to find a comfortable place to read. The place I choose to read depends on the nature of what I am reading. If I am reading literature, history, or social studies in general, I like to sit in a big easy chair where I can relax. On the other hand, if I am reading a mathematics or science book, I sometimes prefer to sit at a desk where it will be convenient to solve problems or take notes. Your favorite reading spot should be one that you associate with sitting down and commencing with your reading, which for some is a library. Your reading spot should also be relatively quiet, so you will not be distracted by noises. If noises are unavoidable, then you may want to play some background music (I like classical music) to drown them out. My only caution is that you do not want to be too comfortable, such as lying down in bed, because your attention may not be as keen and you may have a tendency to fall asleep. Finding the right spot is a personal matter, so I will leave it up to *you*.

An important aspect of finding a comfortable location to read is having the proper lighting. If you sit in a dark corner without adequate lighting, you may tire easily or even damage your eyes. I recommend that you read under fluorescent lighting rather than a bright lamp because you will stay more alert. Fluorescent bulbs that fit into a standard lamp can be readily purchased, and will last longer and lower your electric bill. Make sure that the light shines overhead or over your shoulder to avoid having a glare in your eyes.

Be sure to wear comfortable clothing, so you will be able to sit in a particular spot for an extended period of time.

Always Preview a Book Before Reading It

Most people pick up a book and start reading from the beginning, but this is the wrong approach. With the exception of novels, in which you do not want to learn too much too soon, always preview a book before you read it. Look the entire book over, starting with the title page, which describes what the book is about. Read the statement about the author, usually located at the back of the book, which has important information about his or her background and experiences. Next, read the preface or foreword, located at the front of the book, which tells why the author wrote it, how it differs from past efforts, and what he or she hopes to accomplish. Following this, look over the table of contents, which lists the various chapters describing how the book is organized and the specific subjects contained in it. This preview will give you a good overall idea of what the book is about.

In a similar manner, you should preview each chapter in a book before actually reading it. If you are reading the first chapter, which is a good place to start unless you are told to do otherwise, flip through all of the pages to see how it is organized and what it contains. As you flip through the pages, read the major headings, minor headings, summary statements, conclusions, or anything else that is in bold print.

Also notice any pictures, diagrams, graphs, or equations. By previewing the chapter in this manner, you will obtain a good idea of how it is organized and its specific content, almost like reading an outline. In addition, you will have sent much useful information to your mind, so you will understand and remember more when you actually read the chapter. You will have a better idea of what comes next, how it fits in with what you have already read, and how everything fits together to convey the entire message. Always preview a chapter in this manner before actually commencing with your reading.

You are now ready to start reading the first chapter, but how you read it will determine how much you get out of it, which is the task to which we now turn.

Ask the Right Questions as You Read

If you are an active reader, as opposed to a passive one, you will ask the right questions as you read, which will help you understand the author's message. Passive readers may read all of the words, but they do not try to figure out what the author is trying to say, how the sentences relate to each other, or how the author's message relates to their own experiences. They are just going through the motions, and their attention shifts to other thoughts, such as, "What am I going to do after school?" "Who is going to win the game tonight?" or "Which outfit or movie should I buy?" In contrast, an active reader asks the right questions to understand the author's central message, how the ideas in the book relate to one another, and how the message relates to what they have learned in school.

What are the right questions that I keep referring to? Very simply, as you read you should ask questions such as, (1) What is the book about? (2) What does it say in detail? and (3) How does the author's message relate to what my teacher said in class? Most important, you should try to answer these questions as you read, because this will give you a deeper and more lasting understanding.

The best way to understand and remember what you have read is to try to relate it to your own knowledge and experiences. The real value of books is not just that they deepen our knowledge, but they often change our view of the world and our behavior. Therefore, ask yourself if what you have read relates to your own experiences and how you view the world. Sometimes this can be difficult, especially if you are a young student who has not had many experiences. In such cases, you may want to pose questions to a parent or other adult who has had relevant experiences. For example, if you are reading history and want to understand views of the public during a particular war, then you might want to talk to someone who had the experience of living through the war. The important point is that by making these comparisons, the new material you are learning will be more meaningful to you, and it will be easier to understand and remember it.

An active reader also asks critical questions, which challenge what the author is saying. For example, see if you can figure out what issues the author is trying to address, and whether his or her statements are based on knowledge, facts, experience, or opinions. Do not accept everything you read as the gospel truth. Ask yourself whether the author has presented the case fairly, or whether it reflects a biased position. Does the author have a vested interest in presenting the case a certain way? Decide whether you agree or disagree with the arguments made. If you disagree, is it because the author has not stated the situation clearly, or not offered any convincing proof for the statements? You may not know the answers to all of these questions, but the simple act of asking them, and trying to answer them, will make you a more critical and discerning reader.

Let's take a brief detour to illustrate the process of asking critical questions to understand what the author is saying so we can evaluate its significance. The following is a statement on the Monroe Doctrine made by President John F. Kennedy at a news conference on August 29, 1962:

> The Monroe Doctrine means what it has meant since President Monroe and John Quincy Adams enunciated it, and that is that we would oppose a foreign power extending its power to the Western Hemisphere, and that is why we oppose what is happening in Cuba today. That is why we have cut off our trade. That is why we worked in the Organization of American States and in other ways to isolate the Communist menace in Cuba. That is why we will continue to give a good deal of our effort and attention to it.

Do you understand the issue President Kennedy is addressing, and can you determine if his statement is based on knowledge, facts, experience, or opinions? Do you think he has presented the case fairly, without any bias, and do you agree or disagree with the arguments he has made? Let's take a closer, more critical, look at the statement.

In this policy statement, President Kennedy clearly stated what the Monroe Doctrine means, and why he invoked it to address an important issue involving Cuba. If you wanted to learn more about the Monroe Doctrine, you could have done some research to learn that the doctrine has been invoked by several presidents at numerous times throughout our history to address crises involving foreign nations encroaching into our hemisphere. The statement by itself does not offer any evidence of the "Communist menace in Cuba," but the historical record clearly shows that on October 14, 1962, American U-2 spy planes photographed the construction of a Soviet intermediate-range ballistic missile site in Cuba, thus precipitating the Cuban Missile Crisis. If the U.S. did nothing, it would have to suffer the threat of nuclear weapons being launched preemptively at close range, and would appear weak in its own hemisphere to other nations. President Kennedy ordered a naval quarantine, in which U.S. ships stopped and searched all foreign vessels entering Cuba, and reached agreement one week later with President Nikita Khrushchev of the Soviet Union to remove the missiles from Cuba. If President Kennedy had launched an air assault on the missile sites, as many military officials and cabinet members had recommended, this could have precipitated a nuclear war. I hope this example illustrates that an active and critical reader learns much more information than the words written on the page.

Active readers ask questions continuously, even after they have finished reading. For example, after you have finished reading a chapter in a book, take a few minutes to quiz yourself mentally on what you have learned. Ask yourself what the author's main message was in the chapter, and review the arguments that he or she made to support it. I am not asking you to memorize what the author wrote, but instead to state it in your own words because this indicates that you really understand something. If you cannot state the message in your own words, in a way that is reasonably close to what the author said, then you have not really understood what you read. This simple exercise will help you make sure that you understand and remember the central message and the various ideas that support it.

Learn to Use a Dictionary Frequently

You will not be able to understand the full extent of the author's message unless you understand all of the words you read. All too often we tend to gloss over words in a passage that we do not fully understand, in the interest of moving forward with our reading. Sometimes we can get close to the meaning of a word by looking at it in the context of other words in a sentence, but this is not a good substitute for looking up words in a dictionary. It is worth your while to stop reading, and look up the words you do not know in the dictionary. Although it takes more time, this is the only way to understand exactly what a word means so you will fully understand the author's message.

When you look up a word in the dictionary, take the time to study the various aspects of all of the information provided. In particular, look at how to spell and pronounce the word, its origin, how it is used as different parts of speech, and its various meanings. Think about whether you have seen the word before, or if it is similar to other words you have encountered. Try to associate the word with something that you do know, or possibly an experience that you have had, because this will make it easier to remember the word. Now try to use the word in a sentence of your own construction, to make sure that you know the proper usage of the word. If the word is a technical term used in a science class and you do not see it in the dictionary, check whether a glossary in the book you are reading provides its meaning.

Think of looking up words in a dictionary as something you will do not only to understand the author's message, but to build your own vocabulary. We start life without knowing any words, and we build up our vocabulary through conversation and books we read, but the process will be much more complete if we learn to use dictionaries. The more words you know, the easier it will be to read additional authors, and you will start using new words in your own speech and when writing essays and answering exam questions. Just think how many words you would now know if you had been looking them up in a dictionary for your entire lifetime, and how much better you would do on the verbal portion of standard-ized tests such as the SAT. In the past, it might have been a hassle to pick up a dictionary to look up a word, but now you can do it through an online dictionary, which makes the pro-cess much easier. Looking up words is not just for students; it is something you should do for the rest of your life. I still do it today. The task will get easier, because the more words you know, the fewer you will need to look up in the future.

Use Additional Methods to Master the Author's Message

I have already discussed the importance of being an active reader to understand the author's message, but there are ad-ditional things you can do that suit your own reading style. The first rule is that you should always read everything that the author presents in the book. Some students read only the words, and skip over other materials such as tables, charts, graphs, and pictures. This is a big mistake, because these ad-ditional materials usually complement the text. The author has included these additional materials to help the reader understand concepts, and if you skip over them you may be missing something essential—something that may even ap-pear on a test! By taking the time to study these visual aids to gain a full understanding of the text, you will understand more of what you read later on.

Sometimes it is difficult to understand the author's mes-sage, even if you have been an active reader, looked up words in a dictionary, and read everything presented. In such cases, you may need to dig deeper, especially if the subject matter is complicated. Start out by reading more slowly, studying one sentence at a time. Pause after reading each sentence and ask yourself how the thought or concept presented relates to what you have already read. If you still cannot understand the author's message, skip over the confusing part and read ahead. If this goes more smoothly, then go back to the part you found confusing and see if it makes more sense within the context of the subsequent sentences you have read. Sometimes the meaning of thoughts can be figured out within the context of other thoughts in a paragraph, in the same way that the meaning of words can be figured out within the context of other words in the sentence.

To achieve a full understanding of the author's message, you should use all of the methods at your disposal that uniquely help *you* to learn most effectively. We all use our faculties to learn in different ways. Some people find that they can learn most effectively through their sense of vision, some rely on their hearing, and some rely on physical motion. For example, some students learn most effectively by reading silently to themselves, others learn most effectively by reading words out loud, and still others do best when they write down a summary of what they have read. You should discover the approach, or combination of approaches, that works best for you. Just be sure that if you are reading out loud that you do not disturb others, or if you are writing things down that they are not in a textbook that has to be returned. If you own the textbook, you can easily write thoughts down in the margin, underline or use a highlighter, or summarize your thoughts on a separate piece of paper if you want to keep your book looking clean.

How will you know when you are mastering the author's message? The surest indication is that you can almost anticipate each next thought that the author presents before you even read it. This means that you have aligned your thoughts with those of the author, and you are grasping the intended message.

Don't Worry About Reading Faster—It Will Come Naturally!

Everyone wants to read faster to get his or her work done, but you should never sacrifice comprehension for speed, because you may miss a lot. The key to reading faster, and still understanding what you have read, is to see more words as your eyes scan across the page. People who can see several words at a time will read faster than people who can see only a single word at a time. As your eyes move across the page you have to stop periodically, so the act of stopping and then starting again will also slow you down. Anything that causes a disruption will slow down your reading speed. Now you know why it is so important to look up the meaning of words in a dictionary. If you recognize a word, you do not have to stop to ponder its meaning, which takes time. It may take more time in the short run to look up the meaning of words, but it will take less time in the long run because you will have more words in your vocabulary.

You should also recognize that books on different subjects should be read at different speeds. If you are reading a news magazine or a light novel, you can usually read very quickly because you can understand the material as quickly as you read it. On the other hand, if you are reading the textbook for a complicated subject in school, such as mathematics or science, you need to read much more slowly to grasp the subject. William Walker's advice in *The Art of Reading* is especially relevant to mathematics and science: "Learn to read slow; all other graces, will follow in their proper places." If you hurry your reading to the next topic without fully understanding what you have read, you will be making things much more difficult for yourself.

As you gain more experience reading and building your vocabulary, you should be able to read faster. Regardless of the length of a reading assignment, make a commitment to read everything the author presents rather than skipping around, so you will not miss anything. Never try to force yourself to read faster than is natural, because you will be concentrating on reading quickly rather than grasping the author's message. Moreover, the act of trying to read too quickly may make you uncomfortable or cause your eyes to tire. The basic principle is to read at a rate that makes you comfortable and enables you to understand everything you are reading. With time and practice, you will read more quickly in a natural manner and understand more of what you have read.

When you know the right way to read a book, not only will you be able to understand the author's message fully, the entire experience will be more enjoyable. Every time you pick up a book to read, you will be like an explorer embarking on a new adventure. Being able to read in an active manner will increase the quality of your reading experience and help you to expand and retain your knowledge. I think you will find that the more knowledge you obtain from reading books, the task of reading additional books will be even more enjoyable because you will have a broader knowledge base and a better understanding of how the world works. You will start to get that special feeling that I get when I look at all the books on my library shelves, because I know that I have made the wisdom in them part of my own.

Now that you know the right way to read a book, make sure that you employ the new techniques you have learned for the rest of this book.

RECAP

The *Right* Way to Read a Book:

1. Find a comfortable place to read.
2. Always preview a book before reading it.
3. Ask the right questions as you read.
4. Learn to use a dictionary frequently.

5. Use additional methods to master the author's message.
6. And don't worry about reading faster—it will come naturally!

The Right Way to Take a Test
(Understand the techniques for taking various types of tests)

Nineteenth-century English author Charles Caleb Colton said, "Examinations are formidable even to the best prepared, for the greatest fool may ask more than the wisest man can answer."

This may be true, but the fact remains that you will have to take many tests to progress through school, so you might as well learn something about the right way to take them. How well you do on these tests will determine the grades that you receive. When you graduate from high school, colleges will review your grades to determine whether you are a serious student who is likely to succeed. And when you graduate from college, prospective employers will review your grades when considering how well you will do in their organization. Therefore, the information in this section is of critical importance if you are to become a successful student.

Even though students may be bright and study very hard for examinations, many do not do well because they are not "testwise," which means that they do not know the special skills required for scoring high on tests. These skills are not always that obvious, but they can be taught. In this section, I am going to teach you the basic skills that will help you do well on any type of test, and the specialized skills that will enable you to do well on particular types of tests. The types of tests I will cover include classroom examinations, such as objective tests (true-false, multiple choice, and fill-in-the-blank), essay tests (written composition), problem tests (in mathematics and science), and open-book tests (which allow you to use additional materials). I will also cover take-home tests, oral tests, and comprehensive written tests.

Before Taking Any Test, Always Do the Following . . .

Always arrive well before the test begins. There are two reasons why you should never be late for a test. First, being late may make you nervous, so you will not be able to perform as well on the test. Second, you may need all of the time you can get to complete the test, so why waste it needlessly?

Bring all of the supplies that you will need. Think ahead of time about what you will need to take the test, such as pencils, pens, erasers, paper, and exam booklets. For a mathematics or science test, specialized equipment such as rulers, compasses, or calculators might also be necessary. You will perform much better if you do not have to worry about what you need to take the test.

Never listen to classmates' guesses about what will be on the test. The simple fact is: They do not know—unless they have cheated, and then you do not want to know! When you walk into the classroom ahead of time to take a test, block out any chatter from your classmates about what they think the questions will be. You will do best by basing your answers on what you know, not what someone else thinks.

Read and listen to the instructions. This one is so important that I am going to say it again—read and listen to the instructions! How are you going to do well on the test if you do not know what you are supposed to do? The written instructions on the test contain very important information, such as what questions you have to answer, whether you must answer them in a certain order, whether you have a choice in what questions to answer, whether the teacher expects a certain type of answer, and how many points will be assigned to each question. Sometimes the teacher will come up with additional instructions that did not get included on the test paper, so it is very important that you listen for these when the test is handed out.

Write your name on the test paper before you begin. Sometimes students are in such a hurry to get started on a test that they forget to write their name on the test paper. Wouldn't you be sorry if you worked very hard on a test and the teacher gave your A to someone else? Just think how hard it would be for the teacher to know which exam belongs to whom on a multiple-choice test in which several students forget to write their name. It happens all the time!

Engrave these five principles about taking any type of test firmly in your mind, so you will do them automatically and never forget them!

The Right Way to Take an Objective Test

Objective tests, which include true-false, multiple choice, and fill-in-the-blank questions, usually are given all through elementary, middle, and high school, and often appear in college classes as well. The basic idea of an objective test is that there is only one correct answer for each question, so everyone is expected to answer the questions in the same manner. Some objective exams test only your ability to remember information, whereas others test your ability to understand, interpret, analyze, and apply your knowledge. Teachers like objective tests because the same standards apply to everyone and they are easy to grade. It usually only takes about a day or two for the teacher to grade and return the papers, and sometimes classmates grade each other's papers immediately after the test is taken. Because of the frequency with which objective tests are given, it is important that you know the right way to take them.

When you are first given an objective test, it is useful to flip through the exam to see the number of pages and questions, but you should not read through all of the questions before marking your answers. The best strategy is to answer the questions in the order that they appear on the exam. If you come across a question that seems very difficult, leave it blank, put a question mark in the margin, and move on to the next question. You can always return to the difficult question later on, and it may become easier once you have had additional time to think about it. In addition, you might have come across other questions that provide clues about the best way to answer the difficult question. Once I was conducting a study seminar for students, and when I made this point the teacher remarked that he often intentionally includes questions on objective tests that provide clues to those that are difficult to answer.

One of the most troubling aspects of the multiple-choice form of objective tests is that several of the available choices seem reasonable, but you know that you can select only one. The best approach is to try to figure out the correct answer after you read the question but before you look at the available choices. You may have confidence in your answer if you see it in the list, but you should still look carefully at the other possible choices to make sure that none seem more correct than your answer. If you do not know the answer after reading the question, examine each of the choices very carefully and eliminate those that you know are wrong. This will help you identify the correct answer through a process of elimination. Obviously, the same approach also works in the true-false form of an objective test, although here you only have to eliminate the false choice. Unfortunately, in the fill-in-the-blank form of an objective test, you either know the answer or you do not, but here again later questions may provide helpful clues to the answer for a difficult question.

One of the most important pieces of advice on an objective test is to avoid superstition, which can come in many forms. You should not think that a pattern like T, F, T, F, T, F on a true-false test means that the next answer must be a "T," or that a pattern like a, b, c, a, b, c on a multiple-choice test means that the next answer must be an "a," because the pattern may end at any time. Also, you should not avoid answers that allow no exception (such as *all, always, must, never, none,* and *only*) in favor of answers that allow some exception (such as *frequently, normally, often, rarely, seldom, sometimes,* and *usually*). And there is no reason why the correct answer is more likely to appear in the middle of the choices rather than at the beginning or the end, or that the shorter or longer choice is more likely to be the correct one. Some people tell you to stick with your first answer to a question because it is likely to be the correct one. All of this is superstition and you should avoid it.

The only sure way to select the correct answer is that you must *know* what is true and what is false! As renowned Dutch philosopher Benedict de Spinoza said, "He who would distinguish the true from the false must have an adequate idea of what is true and false."

There is one more piece of useful advice in objective exams, and it involves making educated guesses. If you have worked your way through the entire exam and you do not know the answers to some of the questions, the best approach is to make a guess. That's right, guess! On a true-false test you have a fifty-fifty chance of being right, and on a multiple-choice test you still have a decent chance of being correct, depending upon the number of options in a question. Even on a fill-in-the-blank test you might as well guess, because if you put down nothing you will surely get zero points on the question. If the teacher imposes a penalty for being wrong (subtracts points), it may still be worth your while to guess if the penalty is small enough.

The Right Way to Take an Essay Test

The essay test is generally the most unpopular form of test with students because it can be so challenging, but more and more teachers are giving them these days, even at the lower grade levels. Teachers like essay tests because they give a true reading of a student's understanding of a subject. Not only can the teacher see your answer to a specific question, but also the reasoning behind your answer. It is not enough to remember information for an essay test, because you must also be able to explain it effectively in your answer. To write a good answer in an essay test, you must be able to think creatively, organize your answer into a structured response, and express it in a very clear and convincing manner. These are skills that you will need in answering essay tests all through school, as well as when writing papers, and most likely a skill you will need when you get a job. Therefore, you should devote some time and practice to make sure that you can write an effective essay.

The most important advice in an essay test is to not be too anxious to start writing the answers to the questions. How you spend the first couple of minutes on the test will determine which questions you will answer, the approach you will use to answer them, how well you will answer them, and the grade you will receive. When the teacher hands out the test, use the first couple of minutes to look over the exam very carefully. Notice the number of pages in the exam and the number of questions on each page. It is important to read all of the questions on an essay test before attempting to answer any one of them. If you try to answer the questions too quickly, you may head off in the wrong direction and waste valuable time and effort.

As you read each question, ask yourself exactly what is being requested. Does your teacher want to know if you understand the basic principles, see the relationship between ideas, or can explain the details? Underline the action words that tell you what you are supposed to do. For example, does the question ask you to *describe* (list the characteristics) or *discuss* (tell what you know); to *compare* (list the similarities) or *contrast* (list the differences); to *demonstrate* (explain through examples) or *develop* (draw a conclusion)? Each of these instructions may sound very similar, but they are asking you to do something quite different. If you do not know the exact meaning of such words, then you will not be able to answer the question to the best of your ability. In "Key Words used in Examinations" (appendix B) at the back of this book contains a list of the action words that are frequently used in essay tests, along with an exact meaning of each instruction.

If you do not understand exactly what a question is asking for, do not be shy about going up front to ask the teacher to explain it to you. Teachers will not think less of you for doing this, because they want to make sure that students understand the questions so they will have a fair chance at answering them.

As you read each question on the exam, write down words or thoughts that come to mind because these will help you to answer the question. You can write these down in the margin of your test paper or on your answer sheet. Do not be concerned at this point about writing out complete sentences, just words or short phrases that will remind you of the thought later when you actually start to answer the question. It is important to read all of the questions on an essay test in this manner before attempting to answer any one of them.

There are three good reasons why you should read all of the questions on an essay test before answering any one of them. First, you will want to know everything that is on the exam so you will not be surprised later. Second, sometimes the essay questions are related to each other, so it is important to know this in advance. And third, by reading all of the questions at the beginning of the test, you will be giving yourself more time to think about how to answer the difficult ones.

After you have read through all of the questions, the first thing to notice is whether you have to answer all of them or have a choice. If the teacher has given you a choice, such as answer any three out of the four listed, then you have to decide which ones you will answer. The common-sense rule is to select the three questions that you know the most about. You should be able to make this determination from the words and thoughts that you wrote down when you first read each of the questions. Do not do something silly such as picking the questions that offer the greatest challenge, because this is not the time to be daring or adventuresome.

Once you have read through all of the questions, notice the number of points you will receive for answering each one. Add these points up, and divide the time available so you will spend a proportional amount of time on each question based on its point score. For example, suppose you have two hours to answer three questions, one worth fifty points and the other two worth twenty-five points each. You should plan on allowing one hour to answer the fifty-point question and a half hour for each of the twenty-five-point questions. You cannot always rely on a working clock on the wall, so wear a wristwatch so you will know when to finish and start each question. Try to stick to the planned schedule so you can finish everything on time and have your best chance at getting the maximum number of points. It will not do you any good to do a masterful job on one of the questions, and botch the other two.

Now you have to decide on the order in which you will answer the questions. If the teacher has already stipulated the order, then you do not have any choice. However, if you do have a choice, then I suggest that you answer the easiest questions first and save the more difficult ones until last. This is a good strategy because by finishing the easiest questions first, you will have more confidence when you return to the difficult ones later on. In addition, you will have more time to think, even if subconsciously, about how to put together a good answer for the more difficult questions.

You are now ready to write your complete answer to the first essay question. When you read the first question at the beginning of the test, you probably jotted down a few words or short phrases that came immediately to mind. Now is the time to develop these thoughts into a complete answer. Think about what you know on the subject, break it down into different parts, and think about the relationship between these parts. If you come up with different possible answers to the question, throw all of the answers out except the best one, which will become *your* answer.

As you go through the process of thinking about your knowledge on a subject, no doubt you will come up with additional information that you can include in your answer. Write this down along with your earlier thoughts. Again, it is not necessary to write complete sentences, only words and short phrases. You should now have all of the major points that will go into your final answer. The next step is to organize these points into an answer that will make sense. You do not have time to write a formal outline, so I suggest that you just number the points in the order that you will present them.

You are now ready to begin writing a complete answer to

the question. The starting point is to recognize that a good essay has a beginning, a middle, and an end. The beginning (or introduction) of your essay should state your theme (or major point or idea) very clearly. The middle (or body) of the essay will develop and support this theme. Each paragraph should contain supporting reasons and arguments. In developing your arguments, you should mention relevant facts, details, examples, and ideas. This will demonstrate that you have both detailed and general knowledge about the subject. It is wise to incorporate some of the things the teacher said in class into your answer, because this will show that you have absorbed some of his or her wisdom. If the essay concerns a technical subject, be sure to use the correct technical terms. The end (or conclusion) of your essay should summarize your theme and state what you have proven.

I have just used several pages describing how to write an essay, but once you understand the process you will be able to run through the main points fairly quickly.

There is one basic rule when writing an answer to an essay question, which students violate all of the time. The rule is: *Answer only the question that is asked!* Avoid writing an answer to the question that you *wish* the teacher had asked. If your answer contains a lot of padding and irrelevant details, the teacher may think that you do not know the answer and are trying to fake it. All of the extra effort will not earn you extra points, and may even cause you to lose points! It is best to use Occam's razor, stated by English Franciscan friar William of Occam: "A plurality must not be asserted without necessity."

Regardless of how much you have studied for a test, you may come up against a question that is just plain baffling. If this is the case, you should at least start to write something. After all, if you have studied for the test, you must know something relevant to the question being asked. (I once had a teacher who said that we are wiser than we know!) As you start to write, think about the major points or themes you studied, and sometimes you will connect with an idea that leads to another idea, and still another, until you have a fairly good answer to the question. One thing for certain is that if you do not write anything, you will not get any points. If you write something, you at least have a chance of getting partial credit, even if the answer was not exactly what the teacher was looking for.

If a question seems too difficult and you do not even know where to start, then do not spend too much time on it. Mark the question, leave enough room for an answer, and move on to the next question. You can return to the difficult questions after you have answered the easy ones, and they may be more manageable because you have had additional time to think about them.

No matter how hard you have worked, or how careful you have been in writing your answers to the essay questions, they will contain some errors. No one is perfect! There may be spelling errors, omitted details, errors in logic, or other problems. Always allow for some time at the end of the exam so you can correct the errors or explain your thoughts in more detail.

In some essay exams, not only do you not have time to spare at the end, you do not even have enough time to answer all of the questions. In such cases, the most important rule is to stay calm. *Don't panic!* If you have run out of time, the best approach is to write a short note to the teacher explaining the situation, along with an outline of what your answer would have contained if you had time to finish. The outline should contain major headings and minor headings, along with some supporting facts and a few key phrases. I think you will be surprised at how many points you will earn because teachers know that anyone can run out of time on an exam. They have probably done it many times themselves!

The Right Way to Take a Problem Test

A problem test is an exam that you take in a subject such as mathematics or science. They test your ability to reason and solve quantitative problems. Even if you are not naturally adept at mathematics, there are certain things that you can do to score high on problem tests. Consider word problems, which usually give students the most difficulty. As with essay tests, you should read through all of the questions on a word problem test before attempting to answer any one of them. As you read each question, underline key pieces of information, such as words that tell you what you are supposed to do, amounts that are given, units of account, and so forth. In the margin of your test paper, or on your answer sheet, write down any formulas that you want to remember or approaches that will be helpful in solving the problem.

After you finish reading the first word problem, you should read each of the additional questions in the same manner. When you have read through all of the word problems, you should have a good idea of the ones that will be easy and those that will present some difficulty. If you are given a choice, always choose the problems that are easiest and figure out how much time you will have to solve each one. As with essay tests, if the teacher does not stipulate an order, always work on the easiest problems first and return to the more difficult ones later on. This will build your confidence because you have already completed a substantial portion of the test, and give you additional time to think about a solution to the really difficult problems.

When you start to work on your detailed answer for each problem, first make sure that you know exactly what you are supposed to do. List all unknowns that you are supposed to find, copy important information given in a table, and write down any additional formulas that will be needed to solve the problem. Sometimes it helps to draw a flow chart or picture that lays out how you plan to solve the problem. Also, it may be helpful if you can predict a reasonable answer to the problem before you start, so you can compare the answer you derive to the one you predicted.

There are two important things that you should always do when writing down your answers to a problem test. First and foremost, *always show all of your work on the paper*. Do not try to perform complicated calculations in your head, because if you take the wrong path or make a silly mistake the teacher can at least see where you went wrong and give you partial credit. If you do not show your work, the teacher has no idea of what was going through your head at the time. Second, *always be very careful about how you do your work*. If you are sloppy or in a hurry, it is very easy to make mistakes when you are doing the calculations. After you finish your work on a particular problem, go back and read the question again to make sure that you supplied all of the information that was requested. It is also a good idea to draw a box around each of the final answers that was requested so it will be easy for your teacher to locate them. You do not want to run the risk of losing points because your answers are buried in a bunch of calculations and the teacher cannot find them.

If you come across a problem that is very difficult to solve, keep your wits about you and do not panic. You may need to employ a slightly different approach to solve such problems. First, think about similar problems that the teacher presented in class, or problems that you did for homework, and the methods that were used to solve them. Sometimes you can use an approach that will make the problem easier to solve, such as substituting one value for another, or collapsing one formula into another. Second, it is sometimes easier to solve a problem if you attack it from a different direction. Remember that there are often several ways to solve a problem, and a different approach may help you avoid several complicated calculations. If you are still having difficulty, it may help to break the problem up into several parts that are easier to deal with separately.

The beauty of problem tests is that you know a correct answer exists. This should give you the energy to be tenacious, and to try different approaches until you arrive at the correct answer. The most important advice is that you should never give up on a problem test. Always write down everything you attempt, and cross it out rather than erase it if it is incorrect, because this will at least show the teacher that you are trying. The partial credit that you get for your efforts may be the difference between an A and a B.

I have described the proper approach for solving word problems, but if you have a problem test that only involves solving equations (as in an algebra test), you do not need to read all of the questions in advance. As with an objective test, solve the equations in the order in which they appear.

The Right Way to Take an Open-Book Test

An open-book test is an exam that you take in class, in which you are allowed to use materials such as books, notes, and "cheat sheets." Sometimes you are allowed to use only certain materials, and other times you can use anything you want. Unlike the other forms of exams we have discussed, which test your ability to understand information, the open-book test also requires you to locate, organize, and present information.

There is one cardinal rule about open-book tests: *Just because you can use additional materials during the exam, this does not free you of the responsibility to study and pre-*

pare for it. You can have all the materials you want, but if you do not know how to use them they will be useless, and may even get in the way. To be successful, you will still need to do all of the assigned readings, and learn how to use the various charts, tables, and formulas, *before* you take the test.

If you are allowed to use a "cheat sheet" on an open-book test, you should put in the necessary time to make sure that it is carefully organized, so it will be effective. You should only include information that you will need on the test, not everything you reviewed in preparation for it. Besides, it is impossible to write everything down on a sheet of paper, and even if you could you would have a hard time locating it during the test. It is wise to create an index that points to specific topics in your textbooks and class notes in an organized manner, to make them easy to locate. Make sure that the details are clearly written and evenly separated, so you will not pick up the wrong information during the test. And, by all means, review your cheat sheet several times before the exam so you will be comfortable with it.

Another important rule about open-book tests is the following: *Make sure that you know exactly which materials can be used during the test.* It would be very disconcerting if you planned to use certain materials during the test, only to find on the day of the exam that they were not allowed. When the teacher says that certain materials can be used on the open-book test, do not be so overconfident that you do not bring them along because you think you know the subject by heart. This may put you at a disadvantage with your classmates who do use the materials, because many exams are graded on a curve.

The Right Way to Take a Take-Home Test
A take-home test is similar to an open-book test, except that you have more time to complete it in the comfort of your own

home. Most teachers give students several days or a week to complete a take-home test, and allow them to use any materials they want. Because of this, the questions asked on a take-home test are typically much more difficult than those encountered on an in-class test; otherwise, almost everyone would get an A.

The biggest mistake that students make on a take-home test is not starting soon enough, resulting in not having enough time to complete the exam. If the teacher allows a full week to complete the test, many students will not start working on it until a day or two before it is due. When they see the difficulty of the test, they begin to get nervous or panic, and, as a result, they do not do their best work.

You should always try to start working on a take-home test as soon as you can. In fact, immediately upon receiving the test, you should read each of the questions carefully to get an idea of what you will be facing. Divide the total amount of time allowed to complete the test by the number of questions asked, taking into account their point score, and plan on devoting a proportionate amount of time in answering the questions so you will finish on time. Do your best to stick to this schedule, and avoid the temptation to procrastinate, because you will be making things more difficult for yourself.

The knack to taking take-home tests is knowing exactly where to look to find the answers to the questions. Because take-home tests are usually a little tricky, you probably will need to look beyond your textbooks and class notes to find the answers. You may need to peruse outside readings, go to the library, or search the Internet, and that is another reason why you should get started early. Now that you know the proper way to preview a book, you can scan through these various sources quickly to determine if they contain information that is relevant to the question you are trying to answer. One final caution: Do not get so excited about looking far that you neglect to look near! It is very possible that the answer is contained in your textbook or class notes, and the question is merely asking you to interpret it in a slightly different way.

The advice I gave on essay tests also applies to take-home tests: *Answer only the question that is asked,* not everything you can think of to fill up space. Here again, you do not want to give your teacher the impression that you do not know the answer and you are trying to fake it. Make sure that you express your answer in your own words, not the words that you lifted directly out of a book. This will show your teacher that you have a good understanding of the material, and also avoid a possible charge that you are guilty of plagiarism.

A final piece of advice is that it is always desirable to type your answers rather than write them, even if not requested. This will make it easier for your teacher to read and understand what you have written, and may even earn you some extra points. And, by all means, if the teacher has requested a typewritten paper, make sure that you adhere to all of the specified conventions.

The Right Way to Take an Oral Test

Although oral tests in class are relatively rare, there are occasions when you will have to take one. Oral exams date back to medieval times, before the invention of the printing press, when students had to be tested orally to evaluate their knowledge. When I was a graduate student in economics, I had to defend my Ph.D. dissertation before six professors and a dean. This was a very important oral test for me, because I had to answer all of their detailed questions before they would grant me the degree. Students who write a term paper are often asked to present their findings to the class. Although this is not an oral test per se, how well you do will probably be a significant part of your overall grade.

If you have to take an oral test, there are several things that you should do to prepare in advance. First of all, talk to your teacher about what is expected in the oral exam. Will you be expected to explain a subject in a broad way, or will you be required to have mastery over the details? Second, find out how long the oral test will likely take, so you will know how much time to put into preparation. Third, find out what the ground rules are, such as whether you will be allowed to ask questions yourself to move the discussion along. Once you know what is expected, take the time to prepare an outline listing the subjects that will likely be covered. Although you may not be able to use any materials when taking the test, preparing an outline in advance will help you structure your thoughts and remember some specifics.

An oral test measures your ability to analyze and integrate information, and to respond quickly in an organized manner. To do this effectively, listen carefully to your teacher's question(s) so you will know exactly what is being requested. If you do not fully understand the question, do not be hesitant about asking for a clarification. As the teacher starts to ask the question, you should immediately start to think about your answer and how you will present it, so you can respond promptly in an organized manner. When giving your answer, look directly into your teacher's eyes, speak in an affirmative tone, and be sure to use the proper pronunciation and technical terms to show that you have mastered the material.

If you are asked a question that you are not knowledgeable about, recognize that you are expected to say at least something rather than sit there with a blank stare on your face. Talk about something that seems related, and perhaps you will connect with a memory chain or get a cue from the teacher that leads you in the right direction. If you still are unable to arrive at the correct answer, do not hesitate to return to the question later in the test if the answer suddenly pops into your mind.

The important thing to realize is that there is nothing particularly unusual or frightening about an oral test. It is just like any other test, but in a slightly different form. The major difference is that you are using your mouth rather than the pencil or pen in your hand to respond. In fact, some of the differences between the two types of tests work to your advantage. You get immediate feedback, and if your answer is off the mark you likely will get an opportunity to modify or change your response. You will use the same techniques to study for an oral test as in any other type of test, which I will be describing in the next chapter.

The Right Way to Take a Comprehensive Written Test

Many teachers or education departments require a comprehensive written examination at the end of a course or curriculum to make sure that their students have mastered the material presented. For example, as part of the requirement for getting a Ph.D. in economics, I had to take four comprehensive written exams lasting a full day each on economic theory and fields that I had selected as a major. Students who take Advanced Placement courses in high school are often required to take a comprehensive written test, as are students who take a variety of courses in college.

The distinguishing quality of comprehensive written tests is that the student can be asked questions on any subject covered throughout the term or curriculum, and is expected to demonstrate an acceptable level of knowledge and mastery of the subject. Because of their breadth and depth, comprehensive exams can seem overwhelming to the student, so it is important to know how to prepare for them.

The first task in preparing for a comprehensive written test is to find out who will be designing the exam. If your teacher is the only person asking the questions, then you can use the techniques that I will present in the next chapter on how to prepare for a final exam. However, if other teachers will participate in designing the test, or if it is a standardized test designed by an outside authority, then you have some additional work to do. You should talk to your teacher about who is designing the test, and find out how to locate additional materials that will be helpful in preparing for it. In many instances, teachers assume the responsibility of preparing their students before taking a comprehensive written test, because they know that they will not look good as teachers if their students do not do well on the test. If you are taking a standardized test, then you may want to get a book on strategies for taking the test from the library or a bookstore.

In preparing for a comprehensive written test, it is important not to get mired down in details. As the old saying goes, "Look at the forest before inspecting the trees." Try to look for the major themes that ran through the entire course or curriculum, and how they relate to each other. It will not be necessary to go back and reread everything for the details, because this may even interfere with your ability to integrate information. Once you have identified the major themes, you can then flesh them out with the relevant details. As you prepare for a comprehensive written test, try to develop a specific point of view and think about the types of questions that might be asked and how you would answer them. Sometimes it is helpful to review the questions on past comprehensive written tests given by your teacher or the educational authority that prepares them. As you do this, it is not necessary to write down answers, but you should think about how you would have answered the questions.

The important point about comprehensive written exams is that they are the way they are described—comprehensive!—so you need to start preparing for them well in advance.

While Taking Any Test, Always Do the Following . . .

Write clearly. It is very important to write clearly on a written exam because you will be helping yourself. Start out by writing your name and other required information very clearly, and practice good penmanship throughout the entire exam. I cannot overemphasize the value of good penmanship. Put yourself in place of your instructor, and imagine having to read several dozen papers written in something resembling chicken scratch. I once had a teacher who said he gave me five extra points on a test because I had written so clearly. Another good reason to write clearly is that your teacher may think you are trying to fake it if he or she cannot read what you have written, which may cost you points. You might find it easier to write a neat paper if you use pencil rather than pen, because you can erase your mistakes rather than mark through them. Organize your responses to the questions very carefully, and make sure that you use complete sentences to express your thoughts clearly. Effective communication is a big part of any written exam, so take pains to use accurate spelling, good grammar, sound paragraph development, and solid theme development, and you will be rewarded accordingly.

After you finish, go back and review your answers. It is always a good idea to go back and carefully review your answers, even if you have finished ahead of time. It is very easy to make a mistake, especially if you have been writing rapidly. Even if you tried to be very careful in answering the questions, several things may have gone wrong. In an objective test, you may have marked the wrong answer or entered it in the incorrect location, so all of the following answers will be out of sequence. In an essay test, your answers may be filled with incorrect spelling, poor grammar, incomplete sentences, poor paragraph construction, or undeveloped thoughts. In a problem test, you may have used the wrong formula, made incorrect calculations, or neglected to show all of your work. All of these types of problems can be easily detected and corrected if you take the time to review your answers after completing a test.

As you go back to review your answers, make sure that you do it in a critical manner. In an objective test, look at the possible choices again to make sure that the one you selected seems more true than the others. In an essay test, ask yourself if you have really given a good answer to the question. If other information comes to mind during your review, be sure to include it in the appropriate places. In a problem test, ask yourself if your answer seems correct, and whether there was a better way to solve the problem. If you have been hurrying to finish an exam you might not have time for a critical review, but if additional time is available it is well worth your while.

Make sure that you use every bit of time available to complete a test. I have taken many exams during my lifetime, and at every one there were students who finished and turned in their papers ahead of time. And in every test, I have heard students complain that they made stupid mistakes that easily could have been avoided. They probably would have caught many of the stupid mistakes if they had just taken the additional time available to review their answers carefully. Do not allow yourself to fall into this trap. The approach I used was that I was the last person to leave the classroom, even if the teacher had to throw me out, because I spent the extra time available making sure that my answers were as good as I could make them. Any product can be made better with additional effort, and an exam is no exception.

RECAP

The *Right* Way to Take a Test:
   Before the test:

1. Always arrive well before the test begins.
2. Bring all of the supplies that you will need.
3. Never listen to classmates' guesses about what will be on the test.
4. Read and listen to the instructions.
5. Write your name on the test paper before you begin.
6. Learn the proper techniques for taking objective tests, essay tests, problem tests, open-book tests, take-home tests, oral tests, and comprehensive written tests.

   During the test:

1. Write clearly.
2. After you finish, go back and review your answers.

The Right Way to Write a Term Paper
(Select a good topic, conduct research, develop an outline, and write it)

Aldous Huxley, one of my favorite English writers, once said, "A bad book is as much of a labor to write as a good one; it comes as sincerely from the author's soul." If I may paraphrase Huxley, a bad term paper is as much of a labor to write as a good one, and that is why you need to learn the right way to write one.

The ability to write is a skill that is important to anyone in our society who is involved in communicating the written word, but is especially important for students. If you think about it, writing is probably the most important form of communication in the business and technical world, because there needs to be a permanent record of anything of importance. You probably do some form of writing every day, even if it does not involve the completion of an assignment for class. Writing is probably the most important form of communication you will have with your teachers in school. Next to reading, you will probably spend more of your time writing than on any other activity. The grades you receive in your classes depend very much on what you write on exams. In virtually all of your classes, except those that are purely quantitative such as mathematics, you will be expected to write essays, reports, book reviews, and term papers. Of all of the various writing assignments, the term paper is one of the most important, yet the one that presents the most difficulty to students. That is why I am concentrating on it here.

You may be wondering why teachers put so much importance on writing term papers. After all, they normally account for about a third or more of your total grade. There are at least three reasons why teachers assign term papers and value them highly. First, they want you to demonstrate that you have learned something about the subject you are studying, and that you can analyze the ramifications of it in a structured and significant way. Second, they know that you will be required to write something later on in life, regardless of the occupation you enter, so they view it as their responsibility to teach you the right skills. And third, term papers present an opportunity for you to demonstrate what you know about a subject, even if you have not done well on examinations or other aspects of the course that are graded.

To write a good term paper, you will need to do several things to show that you have investigated a subject in detail. First, you will have to demonstrate that you have used the proper methods to research a subject. This may involve use of the library to collect books and articles relevant to the subject, or an extensive search of the Internet to find additional sources of information and applications. Next, you will need to show that you can organize the information you have collected into a well-structured format that develops the important ideas and themes. Finally, you will need to prepare a well-written term paper that uniquely contributes ideas and recommendations of your own. These are the steps that any author, such as myself, must go through when writing a book, and they are essentially the same steps that you will need to go through when writing a term paper, whatever the subject. Now let's develop them in detail. I will divide them up into several specific tasks.

Select the Right Subject for Your Theme

It is important to select the right subject for the theme of your term paper, because you will be spending a lot of time and effort writing it. You should select a subject in which you have always been interested, or perhaps a subject the teacher mentioned in class that caught your attention. The subject should be relatively narrow rather than broad, or you may not be able to deal with it adequately in the time and space available to write the paper. If you are having difficulty selecting the right subject, you can start off with something broad and then narrow it down as your work progresses. If you are still having difficulty selecting the right subject, do not hesitate to ask your teacher for a suggestion.

Ask Specific Questions to Develop a Theme

After you have decided on an appropriate subject for your paper, you need to ask specific questions to develop a relevant theme. The reason specific questions are important is that you will need to know what you are looking for when you conduct your research. Your questions may be very broad at this point, and they may change over time as you narrow them down. Basically, your questions should involve the same types of information that a reporter seeks when writing an article on a subject—who, what, where, when, how, and why? Write your questions down so you will not forget them. As your work progresses, you may modify your questions further or come up with additional ones. If you are having difficulty identifying specific questions at this early stage, ask your teacher for suggestions. This has the added advantage of revealing what your teacher thinks is important, so your paper will reflect work on a subject that the teacher thinks is worthwhile.

Conduct Your Research in a Systematic Manner

Once you have developed specific questions for your term paper, you will need to conduct research to find the information to answer them. Most likely the information will be located in books and articles on the subject. Sometimes teachers mention or list relevant books and articles when they assign a subject or help a student decide on one. Each book and article may have references that will help you find additional sources on related subjects. If you still do not have enough materials to read, you can ask your teacher for additional suggestions.

A library is the best place to find the books and articles you need, or to identify additional ones. Unlike the days when I was a student, and had to spend hours searching through card catalogs, most libraries permit you to find the materials you need by searching through the library's virtual catalog, using your own computer in the comfort of your own home. Most systems will tell you if the book or article is carried, whether it is on the shelf and available for checkout, and some even allow you to reserve or check out the book or article online. If the material you need is in the reference section, you may be able to save or print it out on your home computer if the length is not excessive. Some library systems are quite sophisticated, and may even give you a listing of related books and articles with a short summary of their content. All of these devices have made modern research much simpler and more efficient than it used to be. If you need assistance in using the automated system at your library, do not hesitate to ask the librarian for help.

The other excellent place to conduct research is over the Internet. By using a few key words on a search engine such as Google, you can literally search the entire world to find the material you are seeking. Many of the entries that are returned in a general search will be the same books and articles that you can check out in the library, although sometimes the material will be available directly online. The use of search engines also makes it possible to locate a variety of information in addition to the basic sources, such as applications involving the subject or views from people who have a similar interest in the subject you are researching. A word of caution is in order, however, because many of the sources on the Internet reflect opinion and results that are not substantiated by science or accepted methods, so you need to be particularly careful in what you select for your own research. Many teachers will insist that you reference only authoritative or recognized sources when you put together the list of references for your own term paper.

Now that you know the right way to read a book or article, you can use these methods when trying to find relevant materials for your research. In the case of a book, it should take you only a few minutes to scan through the table of contents, major headings, summaries, and illustrative graphs and charts to determine if it contains information relevant to your research. In the case of an article, you can scan through the abstract (which is a short summary of the article), the introduction, and the conclusion to determine if it is relevant.

Once you have found a book or article that is relevant to your research, you should take very careful notes on what you read. You should try to take notes only on passages that are relevant to your research, not everything you read; otherwise, you may end up with an overabundance of material that will be less than useful. As American psychologist-philosopher William James said, "The art of being wise is the art of knowing what to overlook." Try to put the information in your own words, rather than copying it word for word, because it will be more meaningful to you when you read it later on. If you see a passage that you want to quote, write it down in the exact words enclosed by quotation marks, review it carefully for accuracy, and document its location.

Whether you are quoting someone directly or just repeating a person's thoughts, it is essential to give the source proper credit. Always record detailed information that you can use in your references and footnotes, such as the name of the author, title of the book, name of the publishing house, where and when it was published, and the page number. If you found information on the Internet, be sure to record the name and location (URL) of the site. It is wise to keep track of this information as you read rather than try to locate it at a later time, which would be a lot of extra work and may even seem impossible.

You will definitely need a good system to keep track of all of the information you gather in your research. A common approach has always been to write all of the information on three-by-five inch index cards or standard-size paper, although many people now record the information on computers. If you are compiling the information by hand, you should write only on one side of the page because you will likely want to move the information around later when you organize your thoughts. Writing on both sides of the page will complicate the process. Be sure to use the same system throughout your research, so you will know what you have and how to locate it.

As you conduct your research, try to come up with creative thoughts that go beyond those of others. To do this you will obviously need to think creatively. The secret to creative thinking is a four-step process: (1) You must have a clear understanding of the questions you are trying to answer, (2) you need to collect as much information as possible to answer these questions, (3) you need to let the information "incubate" in your mind for a period of time to come up with possible answers to the questions, and (4) you need to compare the various possible answers with the original questions to decide on the best solution. Be sure to write these answers in your notes so you will not forget them. The creative process is not easy, but reading widely will help you understand what others have done, and even give you some ideas about what has not been done that is relevant to the questions you are trying to answer.

As you conduct your research, the nature of your questions may change. For example, the general questions may have become more specific, or you may have thought of new questions. This is entirely natural, and even exciting, because you always learn more from research than what you originally expected.

Develop an Outline to Organize Your Thoughts

An outline is essential for writing a good paper because it shows you how to organize your thoughts and lays out the order in which to present them. As you conducted your research, you surely noticed that the information can be grouped in some manner that makes sense, such as *when* (the time) it happened, *where* (the location) it happened, or *how* (the order) it happened. The purpose of an outline is to put this information into an ordered structure.

I recommend the conventional structure for outlines: The title of the outline should be the same as the title of your paper; major subjects should be indicated by Roman numerals (I, II, III, . . .); minor subjects should be indented within major subjects, and indicated by capital letters (A, B, C, . . .); additional information should be indented within minor subjects, and indicated by Arabic numerals (1, 2, 3, . . .) and small letters (a, b, c, . . .), as appropriate. Do not forget the conventional rule that any subdivision should have at least two levels (such as A and B or 1 and 2) to be shown.

There are a few simple rules to follow that will help you prepare a good outline. Make sure that your outline has a beginning (the introduction), a middle (the body), and an end (the conclusion). To develop each section, use short phrases that describe the major ideas, not complete sentences that you would use in your final paper. This will make it easier to have a complete look at all of the information you have gathered and see how it is arranged. Remember, the whole idea of an outline is to enable you to see the best way to organize your thoughts. You can see how the various subjects relate to one another, whether you have repeated or contradicted yourself, and where to insert new ideas. It may take you a while to create a good outline, but it will greatly simplify and improve the writing process later on.

After you have completed your outline, the next step is to index all of the information from your research into the appropriate location in the outline. If you have done your research on a computer, print out your notes on only one side of the page, for the reasons mentioned earlier. If you have written your notes on paper or index cards, you are ready to proceed to the next step. Spread out all of the information on the floor or a large table so you can see what you have to work with. Now write the letter or number from the outline on the appropriate page (or portions of pages) of the notes you took when conducting your research. This will give you the ability to see what goes where in the paper. In the process, you will no doubt discover that you have some information that is redundant, which you will need to exclude or consolidate. No doubt, you will also discover that you have neglected to obtain information on some subjects, which you may need to research further.

Write the First Draft of Your Paper

To write the first draft of your paper, all you need to do is to insert the indexed information from the previous step into the appropriate location in the outline, and express the thoughts in complete sentences and paragraphs. I strongly suggest that you do this on a computer, using a good word processor that will enable you to edit and move things around during the process.

The beginning, or *introduction,* of your paper is very important because this is where you will tell readers what your paper is all about, and generate enough interest so they will want to read further. The introduction should state the major questions that you will examine, and provide some clues about how you plan to address them. Some writers also like to state their major conclusions in the introduction, as a way of giving the reader a focal point as the arguments are presented in the body of the paper. The important point about the introduction is that it should be short and to the point, because readers will be anxious to get into the body of the paper if you have succeeded in piquing their interest.

It is often difficult to write an introduction when you first begin the paper, because you do not know everything you will include. Some writers prefer to write their introduction after they have finished the paper and know how everything turned out. My preference is to write at least something for an introduction before beginning the main body of the paper. I then go back to the introduction after I have finished the paper, and make the necessary modifications. Writing at least something for the introduction when you begin the paper will get you warmed up for writing the rest of it.

The middle, or *body,* of the paper is where you fully present your arguments and defend them. To write the body of the paper in the first draft, all you have to do is merge your notes into the proper places in the outline you have developed. The major headings in your outline will become the major subjects or chapters in your paper. The minor headings in your outline will become the subdivisions of the major headings or chapters. The notes that you took from all the readings you did while conducting research fill out the paper in their respective places under the major and minor headings. To improve readability, make sure that your headings stand out in bold or oversized print with the proper levels of indentation, just as I have done in this book.

The most important advice for writing the body of the paper is to observe the rules of good writing.

The *first* rule concerns good grammar and spelling. Make sure that you use complete sentences with proper grammar. Avoid excessive contractions in words (unless you are doing it for effect) and slang. Make sure that you use the parts of speech correctly in your sentences, and that all of your words are spelled correctly. After you write a sentence, look at it critically and ask yourself, "Does this really communicate the idea I want to express effectively, or is there a better way to say it?" It is better if *you* do this type of editing, rather than your teacher.

The *second* rule concerns good paragraph construction. The first or second sentence in the paragraph, which is called the topic sentence, should describe the main idea that will be expressed in the paragraph. Everything else that is included in the paragraph should relate back to the main idea in the topic sentence. All of the other sentences in the paragraph should support the topic sentence through the use of facts, statistics, and examples. These provide the evidence to support your arguments. After you finish writing a paragraph, it is always wise to revisit your topic sentence to see if it could have been written more succinctly or clearly.

The *third* rule relates to good theme development in how you present your ideas. It is essential to present your paragraphs in a manner that will help the reader understand your story. I have a favorite saying that I learned from one of my teachers that concerns the order of things: "Putting on socks and then shoes is very different from putting on shoes and then socks." When you present things in the right order, it will be easier for the reader to follow your ideas and understand your message. Include transitions that will help the reader move more easily from one idea to another. In addition, your paragraphs, and the sentences within them, should not all be of the same length, or your writing will become boring or appear stilted.

The ending, or *conclusion,* is where you summarize the major findings of your paper and leave the reader with a final thought. The conclusion should refer back to the introduction and answer the important questions that were raised there, and also address other important information that was discovered in the process. You should summarize what you have found in the paper, and point the way for additional research that needs to be conducted, perhaps in another paper. The conclusion is your opportunity to leave a final thought with readers, so make sure that they understand and will remember your main message after they put your paper down and move on to something else.

When you are writing the first draft of your paper, try to make it as close to the final version as possible. In other words, practice the three rules of good writing. This will reduce the amount of work you will have to do later on. Also, it is very important to be flexible when reviewing your first draft. Be willing to make changes that make sense, and do not forget to modify your outline to be consistent with what you end up with as your first draft.

After you have finished writing your first draft, let it sit for a while before attempting to write anything further. While the paper sits, you may come up with additional thoughts that will make the paper better. It is not necessary to revise the first draft at this point, but be sure to write these thoughts down so you will not forget them. When no additional thoughts are forthcoming, you will be ready to write the final version of your paper.

Write the Final Version of Your Paper

No matter how accomplished you think you are as a writer, it is always necessary to write a final version of your paper. The first draft may have looked very good initially, but as you begin to rewrite it you will notice problems. Even seasoned writers may need to write multiple drafts. It is similar to the process that artists go through when creating a painting. As the image takes shape, they may paint over portions they don't like, or add fresh details.

Like artists, writers may also need to review their work several times before they are satisfied with the final result. In the process, they may be removing words, sentences, and paragraphs, modifying what they have written so it will read more clearly, or adding new thoughts that were previously left out. Everything in the paper is fair game for change, including the introduction, body, and conclusion. This may seem like you are writing the paper over again, but it could be the difference between writing an average paper as opposed to a good or excellent paper.

When writing the final version of your paper, always be sure to use the particular style that your teacher asked you to follow. If your teacher has asked you to type the paper on standard-size bond paper with one-inch margins all the way around, then do it. If your teacher has asked you to show your footnotes at the bottom of each page rather than at the back of the paper, then do it. If your teacher has asked you to use a certain style when listing your references, then do it. These are small concessions on your part, and they may make the difference between receiving an A or a B on the paper. After all, teachers are reluctant to give a perfect score on any paper, and they are always looking for ways to deduct points. Do not make the process easy for them!

Start Working on Your Paper Early

By now it should be clear that in order to finish all of the steps I have outlined, you need to start working on your paper as soon as possible. In fact, start thinking about your paper as soon as you receive the assignment. As far as the amount of time to spend on each of the steps, plan on spending about half of your time selecting a good subject, asking specific questions, and conducting your research, and the other half of your time developing an outline, writing a first draft, and putting the paper into final form. If you do not start working on the paper as soon as you receive the assignment, all of the steps will get compressed and you will not have time to complete each of them to your satisfaction.

I think most students tend to procrastinate before beginning a term paper, more than before any other assignment they receive in school. Either they think they will have plenty of time to get everything done because the deadline is far removed, or they fear that they will have writer's block if they begin right away. Avoid falling into this trap. The time available is always shorter than you might think, and the best cure for writer's block is to sit down at your desk or computer and just *start writing*!

If you begin early enough, I think you will find the entire process to be more interesting and enjoyable. After all, it is very satisfying to learn more about a particular subject, come up with some new ideas that others had not thought about, and see them expressed in a paper of your own creation. Your teacher will recognize your efforts and reward you with a good grade. And if a college or graduate school asks you for a sample of your writing, you will have something that you are proud to submit.

RECAP

The *Right* Way to Write a Term Paper:

1. Select the right subject for your theme.
2. Ask specific questions to develop the theme.
3. Conduct your research in a systematic manner.
4. Develop an outline to organize your thoughts.
5. Write the first draft of your paper.
6. Write the final version of your paper.
7. Start working on your paper early!

RECAP

The *Right* Way to Read a Book (pages 133–145):

1. Find a comfortable place to read.
2. Always preview a book before reading it.
3. Ask the right questions as you read.
4. Learn to use a dictionary frequently.
5. Use additional methods to master the author's message.
6. And don't worry about reading faster—it will come naturally!

The *Right* Way to Take a Test (pages 145–167):
Before the test:

1. Always arrive well before the test begins.
2. Bring all of the supplies that you will need.
3. Never listen to classmates' guesses about what will be on the test.
4. Read and listen to the instructions.
5. Write your name on the test paper before you begin.
6. Learn the proper techniques for taking objective tests, essay tests, problem tests, open-book tests, take-home tests, oral tests, and comprehensive written tests.

During the test:

1. Write clearly.
2. After you finish, go back and review your answers.

The *Right* Way to Write a Term Paper (pages 167–180):

1. Select the right subject for your theme.
2. Ask specific questions to develop the theme.
3. Conduct your research in a systematic manner.

4. Develop an outline to organize your thoughts.
5. Write the first draft of your paper.
6. Write the final version of your paper.
7. Start working on your paper early!

A System for Getting Straight A's

(A proven ten-point study system that will put you on the road to success)

Marcus Aurelius, one of the most knowledgeable and famous of the Roman emperors, said, "Look to the essence of a thing, whether it be a point of doctrine, of practice, or of interpretation." That is what I have done in developing a system of study for making straight A's in school.

You may have heard some of my ten steps for success in school before, but the essence of my study system is the way these ten steps come together to make a complete system of study. My study system is designed to help you understand everything that your teachers present in class and that you cover in your assignments, so you will be able to achieve the highest possible grades. Although I developed my study system while attending graduate school in economics, I have adapted my study methods so they will apply to any level in school.

I start off my system by discussing the educational curriculum. The educational curriculum is very important, because the courses you take and how well you do in them play a large role in determining how far you will go with your education. I help you to plan a course of study, emphasizing the courses that will enable you to get into college and succeed once you are there. Of the various courses you take in school, I emphasize the importance of mastering English and mathematics, because a thorough understanding of these two courses will help you succeed in every other course you take, regardless of your educational level.

Much of my study system revolves around the importance of teachers as partners in the learning process. Your teachers are the ones who give out assignments, grade your tests and papers, and determine how far you will go with your education. At the lower levels, your teachers are instrumental in giving you the basic knowledge that you will need to succeed at the higher levels. Your professors in college have spent the better part of their lives studying the concepts and principles of a particular discipline. They have devoted years and years working and reworking these concepts and principles into a form that best captures the essence of a subject. When they deliver their lectures in class, they are not just presenting one way of understanding a subject, but what they feel is the best way.

If you can understand everything that your instructors present in class, they will be impressed that you have mastered in one semester or term what it has taken them a lifetime to accumulate. That will get you an A every time, and that is why I put so much emphasis on mastering what teachers present in class.

Because most teachers test students on material they cover in class, my system positions you to learn the most from your teachers. At the lower grade levels (in high school) I show you how to interact effectively with your teachers, and at the higher grade levels (in college and graduate school)

I show you how to choose your instructors so you will have capable and cooperative partners in learning. Some of my rules are very simple, like not missing any classes or sitting in the front row, so you will not miss any material and you will stay focused when you are in class. Others require much more work on your part, such as doing homework and reading assignments before attending class, so you will understand the most from what your teachers present in class.

My system emphasizes taking good notes when teachers are lecturing because this is the best way to understand the material presented in class. As you continue in your education, you will find that the subjects become progressively more complex, and good notes are important not only for understanding but remembering what was presented. I show you the best techniques for taking notes in class, and how to review and supplement them after class, so you will be sure to understand your teachers' lessons. Moreover, by doing this work as your classes progress, you will have started studying for tests ahead of time, which will make you that much better prepared later on when you sit down to take a test.

The most important aspect of taking tests is to have a good idea of what will be on them before you sit down to take them. I show you how to figure out the questions that your teacher is likely to ask, so that you can prepare in advance. This will make tests seem easier and enable you to score higher. I also distinguish the differences between tests given during the regular term and final exams, so you will know how to approach each type of test.

The basic idea of my study system is to teach you everything you need to know to become a straight-A student. You will know exactly how much time you need to put into each aspect of studying and how to use your time most efficiently. Once you have gone through these steps, you can put away your notes and books, and you will not have to worry if you have done enough to prepare for an exam. You will be confident ahead of time that you will make an A on the test, and the only question you will ask yourself is, "How high will it be?" When you reach this level, you will find school more rewarding, and dare I say it—even more fun!—than you ever dreamed possible!

1. Plan a Course of Study
(And always take the right subjects)

Victorian-era English playwright W. S. Gilbert, of Gilbert and Sullivan fame, wrote the following in his play *Iolanthe:*

> *When I went to the bar as a very young man,*
> *(Said I to myself—said I),*
> *I'll work on a new and original plan,*
> *(Said I to myself—said I)*

Whether you are in high school, college, or graduate school, you need to work on a "new and original plan" of what you want to do with the rest of your life so you can take the right subjects to accomplish your goal.

Having a plan of what you want to do with the rest of your life will help you stay focused in school and give you the incentive to work hard. It is always easier to work hard at something when we know that it has meaning and purpose, rather than something we have to do because we are told to do it. Some people know what they want to do with their life at a very early age. Many do not know what they want to do when they enter college, and end up changing their major several times while in college as they search for an answer. And many people change their careers several times during their lifetime because they do not like what they are doing at work and are still searching for the answer. That is why it is wise to begin this process as soon as possible.

High School

Because it may take many years to decide on a career, I advise you take the types of courses in school that will give you the most flexibility later on. Most schools group subjects into different programs with names such as the "academic program," "technical program," and "general program." The academic program has the more advanced and challenging courses, and is used to prepare students for college and professional careers. The technical program has courses that deal with practical applications such as working with machinery and building materials, and is used to prepare students for careers in these fields. The general program includes the basic courses that you need to graduate from high school, but does not include the more difficult courses in mathematics, sciences, and foreign languages.

I would recommend that you enroll in the academic program because it will prepare you for college and lead to better jobs once you get out of school. If you find the academic program too difficult, or decide that you would rather be in the technical or general program, it is always easy to switch into them. It is much more difficult to switch from the technical and general program into the academic program, because you will not have taken the basic courses to understand the material in the academic program. Therefore, I encourage you to remain in the academic program even if you are having difficulty, and use the techniques in this book to make it easier.

Early in the school year, you (and perhaps your parents) should meet with the guidance counselor in your school to find out what courses are included in the academic program. Specifically, find out what courses you will be taking during the rest of the school year and in future years. Inquire about the options for taking the more advanced courses, called Advanced Placement courses, which allow you to earn college credits while you are still in high school. These courses will not only give you better preparation for entering college, they will reduce your workload once you are there. I would encourage you to take as many Advanced Placement courses in high school as you think you can handle and still do well. It is wise to look through the entire program to see where it is heading, so you will know how many credits you will have when you graduate.

It is very important in the academic program to take courses in the proper order. For example, you would not want to take Algebra II before taking Algebra I, and you would not want to take calculus before completing both algebra and trigonometry. Similarly, you would not want to take an advanced course in a foreign language before completing a basic one in it. In most cases, it is hard to get into difficulty because you can only take courses in a certain order, one course a prerequisite for the next; however, if there is an option, make sure that you inquire about the best order to take the courses. Never take courses out of order solely because you are interested in them or think you can handle them, because you may be making your life more difficult than it needs to be—and you may get a poor grade!

If you are taking all of your courses in the proper order and still having difficulty with your studies, then you may need to take a closer look at your abilities as a student. You may not have learned enough from a previous course in the sequence, and that is why you are having difficulty with the current course. Or you may have transferred from another school or state that was not as advanced in its coursework, and that is why you are having difficulty in your present setting.

Fortunately, there are a number of things you can do to remedy such problems. Reading this book will certainly put you on a path to correcting many of these problems, but you may need additional help. For example, if you are having difficulty with reading, writing, or comprehension, you may want to contact your guidance counselor for assistance. Many of them have tests that will determine which of your skills need improvement. Some schools have reading and study skills laboratories with materials that will help you read faster, write clearer, and understand more of what you have read. Most of these services are offered without charge, and it is foolish not to take advantage of them if they are available and you truly need them. Alternatively, you could obtain additional help by enrolling in a learning center, many of which are advertised in the media or on the Internet. They will charge you a fee for their services, but the expense may be worthwhile if you are really struggling with your studies.

College and Graduate School

The first thing you should try to do upon entering college is decide on your major field of study. It is to your advantage to decide quickly, because if you designate several majors with multiple requirements, you may end up taking more courses and spending more time and money on college than you had originally planned. If you are having difficulty deciding on a major, as I did when I was in college, then you should think about the type of occupation you would like to enter so you can take the proper coursework.

There are several things you can do to think about the occupation you would like to enter. I suggest that you read (or reread) chapter 5 in part 1, because it explains how to use online resources that will tell you the characteristics of various jobs and the amount of formal training that you need to enter them. Do not forget to check with the counseling center at your college or university, because they often have useful information on the characteristics of jobs and job availabilities. You may even find a part-time or summer job that will acquaint you with a particular field, and earn yourself some additional money at the same time.

If you are still having difficulty deciding on a specific major, then you should at least make an attempt to decide on a general area of study. Many curricula have a lot of flexibility in the first two years, and allow you to fulfill general requirements that will count toward a degree in any number of fields. This will enable you to postpone your decision on a specific major, without losing your investment on required coursework.

Once you have decided on a field of study, normally you are assigned to an adviser in your department who will help you develop a schedule of courses. Most college programs require a certain number of courses in a wide range of fields, including English, social studies, mathematics, sciences, fine arts, and so forth. You are also allowed to take a number of electives. These course requirements and electives are normally taken during the first two years of study, to allow sufficient time for you to concentrate on your major field of study during the last two years. If you are planning to go to graduate school, make sure that you take the courses during your last two years as an undergraduate that will help you prepare for the graduate level.

As you plan your schedule of courses, it is important to take them in the correct order. Many of the higher-level courses require knowledge of the material presented in lower-level courses. It is similar to building a house: You need a good foundation before erecting the walls and roof, or the house will not stand. Most of the courses listed in college catalogs show the prerequisites for taking courses, but this may indicate a bare minimum of preparation rather than what is desirable. The best approach is to ask your adviser, professors, and other students about the level of preparation needed for a course before you sign up for it. If you take courses out of sequence, without the necessary preparation, you may unnecessarily be making things difficult for yourself.

If you are weak in a specific subject, or lack confidence, it may be a good idea to take a lower-level course before attempting an advanced one. This advice is especially relevant to adults returning to college after an absence of several years. If you did not do well in algebra or trigonometry several decades ago, you may want to go back and retake these courses before attempting a calculus course. Over long periods of time, the content and method of presentation of course material often change, so a refresher course will be time well spent.

If you enroll in a course that is more difficult than you thought, do not be stubborn and try to tough it out if the material really is over your head. Drop the course before you are penalized! As Confucius, the ancient Chinese sage, said, "When you know a thing, to hold that you know it; and when you do not know a thing, to allow that you do not know it— this is knowledge."

You need to be especially careful when signing up for electives because you may get in over your head. You may have an interest in taking an upper-level course in philosophy or literature, but first make sure that you are adequately prepared before registering for the course. If other students in the class are majoring in these subjects, you may be at a serious disadvantage when competing against them on examinations. If your desire to take such courses is very strong, you may want to take some lower-level classes for background before enrolling in the upper-level courses. I learned the lesson the hard way as an undergraduate, when I took an

upper-level course for credit in medieval history without
having any background on the subject. If your school offers pass-fail options for electives, then you can risk being
more venturesome without endangering your grade-point
average.

Once you have planned a course of study, try your best to
stick with it so you can advance toward your degree. However, if you find that you are in the wrong field, then by all
means change your major to get into the right field. If you
dislike a field as a student, then it is highly unlikely that you
would enjoy the field as a career. It does not make any sense
to spend your time and money training for a field that would
bring you a lifetime of unhappiness. Sadly, too many people
have already made that mistake!

Most of my remarks have been directed to undergraduate programs, but they also apply to graduate studies. You
would not want to take higher-level graduate courses before
having the basic courses to serve as foundational material.
However, knowledge about the proper sequence of courses is
generally more pervasive among graduate students than for
undergraduates. The key difference between the two is that
graduate-level study requires much greater commitment than
undergraduate study. Graduate courses are much more complex than undergraduate courses, and the reading lists are
far more extensive and specialized. In addition, you can expect a much higher level of competition from your fellow
students, because they are generally among the brighter students who graduated from college. You should only enroll in
a graduate program if you have a keen interest in the subject
and are willing to do a lot of hard work.

Always Take the Right Subjects

Of all the courses you can take in school, English and mathematics are unquestionably the most important for your

success as a student. That is why you are required to take courses in these two subjects all through school, from the lowest to the highest levels. English is essential because it is the language that we use to think, speak, read, and write. You may know a great deal about the various subjects you take in school, but your teachers will never find out how much you know if you cannot express yourself clearly in assignments and tests. While basic mathematics is essential for functioning in the everyday world, if you do not have a knowledge of higher mathematics you will have a hard time understanding the physical sciences. When people say that science courses are hard, what they really mean is that the mathematics is hard, because you need a full understanding of higher-level mathematics to grasp the subjects presented in most science classes.

In fact, I would go as far to say that if you have a thorough understanding of English and mathematics, then all of the other subjects in the curriculum will be that much easier. Never pass up the opportunity to take another English or mathematics course, regardless of your level in school.

In today's world, I would be remiss if I did not mention that computer science is a very important subject to take in school. Whether in high school, college, or graduate school, you will find that you need to use computers to do the basic work in many classes, and they are now used extensively in many of the laboratory courses offered in school. You will find that computers are used in practically any occupation you enter, from the most rudimentary to the most complex. In fact, you will probably need to know how to use computers to even be considered for many jobs, and this will become even more the case in the future. That is why so many computer courses are offered in the curriculum, and why some knowledge of computers is required in practically every field, even in subjects that are nonquantitative.

You should take as many computer courses as you can fit into your program, whether they involve learning how computers work, writing computer programs, learning how to use the Internet, understanding computer ethics, or even learning how to type. The more knowledge you have about computer science, the greater the advantage you will have when competing with students in the classroom and colleagues at work.

RECAP

Plan a course of study by:

1. Thinking about the occupation you would like to enter
2. Taking the courses that will enable you to enter this occupation
3. Taking the courses in the right order

And always take the right subjects:

1. English
2. Mathematics
3. Computer science

---

2. Choose Your Instructors If You Can
(But always work with your instructors if you cannot)

In the Book of John in the Bible, Jesus told his disciples, "Ye have not chosen me, but I have chosen you." Teachers do not get a choice of the students who will be enrolled in their classes, but students sometimes get a choice of who will be their teachers.

The opportunity to choose your teacher generally arises in college and graduate school, when registering for classes, and not in high school where students are assigned to classes. If you can choose your teacher you should not pass up the opportunity, because it could make a significant difference in your success as a student. At the lower grade levels, when you cannot choose, you still need to work with your teacher, because he or she is your most important partner in learning.

High School

The most important thing that students at any grade level need to understand is that teachers are their friends. That's right—I said "friends." Your teachers are your friends in learning because they give you valuable knowledge about a subject that is important, and likely will become even more important to you in the future. What you need to understand is that teachers give you their special knowledge about subjects because they know you will need it later on, and it will help you succeed not just in higher levels of school but in life.

The best way to work well with your teachers is to get to know them as persons—and the best way to get to know them as persons is to get interested in their subjects. Now you may say that this will not be easy because you are just not interested in English, mathematics, science, history, and the multitude of other subjects you have to take in school. You may also say that you do not see how these subjects will help you later on in life, and I must admit that I had some of the same feelings when I was in high school. As you get older, you will come to realize that *all* of the subjects you take in school are important, and you probably will need to know and use the information in them at some point later on in your life. Moreover, you need to realize that school provides you with a special opportunity to learn about these subjects, and you may not get that opportunity again.

Take a few minutes to think about what is involved in being a teacher. Most teachers are highly gratified from helping their students understand a subject that they feel is important. They know that some of the students they are teaching will be the leaders of tomorrow, so there is a lot at stake in what they teach them. As American historian and academic Henry Brooks Adams said, "A teacher affects eternity; he can never tell where his influence stops." With all of the education they have acquired, teachers could probably work in a number of different fields that pay substantially more money, but they remain teachers because they love their profession.

Students who are working very hard need to realize that their teachers are probably working even harder than they are. Teachers have to attend college for many years to earn degrees in their field of interest, and then have to take a number of education courses to become certified as a teacher. You may see your teachers for only an hour or so each day in class, but they had to spend many hours reading about their subject, preparing their lectures, and grading your papers and tests, in addition to all of the administrative duties that the school assigns to them. Most teachers spend substantially more than a normal workweek to complete all of their duties, and those who are very serious and committed to their subject may be spending most of their time working for you.

When you hear your teachers lecture about their subject in the classroom, you are observing what they think is the best way to present it for you to understand it. After all, teachers have spent years and years studying a subject and they know what helped them to understand it, so they think a similar approach will work for you. If you can get on the same wavelength as your teachers and understand their message, they will be impressed that you have learned in a short time what has taken them years to master. This will separate you from other students in the classroom.

Now that you know where your teachers are coming from, you can concentrate on the best ways to work with them. There are three ingredients in working well with teachers: (1) Show respect, (2) get to know them as persons, and (3) understand their style in the classroom.

It is important to always show respect for your teachers, and let them know that you think their subject is important. The way to show respect is by being genuinely interested in their subject, always working hard, turning assignments in on time, and not speaking out of turn in class. A good way to show your interest is to volunteer when the teacher asks if someone will assume a particular duty. Showing respect means not making any noise or causing any trouble in the classroom. If you create a bad impression it may take substantial time and effort to regain respect, which you may not be able to recover.

Teachers are people, just like your parents and relatives, so spend some time getting to know them as a person. After class, when it is convenient, talk to your teachers about their subject and the other things they are interested in. Tell them more about yourself, what you find interesting about their class, and other things you are interested in. You may find that you and your teachers have many similar interests, and you will start to think of them in a different light. Contrary to what some students may think, this is not "brown-nosing," and if you hear such a remark you should simply ignore it. It is merely an effort to learn more about your partner in learning, which will help both of you succeed in your mission.

It may take some time to learn about your teachers' styles in the classroom, but this will certainly help you work more effectively with them. Different teachers have different likes and dislikes, and no two of them are exactly alike, so you need to spend some time and effort learning about all of them. For example, if your teacher does not like students to be late to class, then do your best to be on time. If your teacher does not like to be interrupted when lecturing, then wait until he or she has finished the presentation before raising your hand to comment or ask questions. If your teacher gets very upset when assignments are handed in late, usually indicated by a deduction of points, then make sure that you always turn yours in on time.

You should do all of these things because your teachers play a special role as your partners in learning. They are the ones who transmit knowledge, make assignments, give tests, and assign grades. They are also the ones who will determine if you get special awards, and whether you are assigned to more challenging classes as your education progresses. They may also be the ones who write that special letter of recommendation that helps you get into the college of your choice. How much you learn, and how far you progress, will be determined in large part by how well you work with your teachers.

College and Graduate School

In college and graduate school, you often have the opportunity to choose your professors for courses, and you should definitely exercise the opportunity. In college catalogs, sometimes a single professor is listed as teaching a class, and sometimes you may be left hanging because who will teach the course reads "to be announced." But the more likely scenario is that several professors will be listed, and you will have a real choice. Be sure that you make your choice based on the quality of professors, and not something trivial such as the times classes are being taught, unless time is an essential consideration for your other activities.

The quality of professors varies considerably, as does any good or service purchased in the marketplace. You should not assume that all professors are good, or even competent, solely on the basis that they are highly educated. The qualities that make a good professor are actually quite straightforward. A good professor will be very dedicated to the profession, cover extensive substantive material during lectures, be fair minded, and be a good communicator.

Now that you know the essential qualities that make a good professor, how do you go about finding the right person? The best approach is to talk to other students and professors because they know who the good ones are. Students who have taken a course from a professor you are considering can give you valuable inside information, such as the content covered in the course, how effectively it is communicated, whether tests are fair and reasonable, and how much work is involved in meeting the requirements of the course. Other professors are often the most informative because they know the discipline and are able to judge other professors more effectively than can students. It is sometimes difficult to get the information from them, however, because they do not want to be undiplomatic by saying something negative about a colleague. Professors are more likely to tell you about other professors who are good rather than bad, and that is why you should only ask about the good ones and not the bad ones.

The most difficult time for you to obtain information about professors is when you first enroll in college. Because you know few of the students and professors, you will have to rely on other sources for information. One source is student newsletters, which occasionally publish the results of student polls on the quality of professors. Another source is Internet sites that provide comments of students who rate their professors. You can certainly learn something from the successes and failures of others, but you should weigh this information carefully. It may reflect the superficial views of students who give low marks to professors who are difficult, and high marks to professors who are easy or humorous. If other students have certain views about professors, ask them to provide an explanation. You can listen to the advice of others, but be sure to make the decision based on your own best judgment.

If you are considering taking a course from a professor, there are other ways to obtain additional information. You could talk to the professor before registering for the class, to get to know him or her as a person and find out specific details about the course. For example, you might be able to get a syllabus, with a course outline and reading assignments, to find out about the content of the course. Many professors provide such information about their courses on the Internet, and some even have their own blogs to discuss subjects of interest with their students. Other useful information is whether the professor assigns homework or requires papers, how many books and articles are used in the course, how many examinations are given, and the specific nature of the examinations. If you have time, you may want to sit in on a lecture or two before you register, to learn more about the abilities of the professor and the content of the course. It takes additional work to obtain this background, but it will provide much useful information on what the professor and the course have to offer.

I am continually amazed at how students can be so selective about some aspects of their lives, and so nonchalant about others. You would not close your eyes when shopping for clothes at the department store. You would not close your eyes and point to the yellow pages to find a doctor to perform a serious operation on your body. So why close your eyes when you hold a schedule of classes and randomly select a professor who will have a big impact on your quality of life for an entire semester? There is a better way, if you just put forth the effort.

RECAP

Choose your instructors if you can, by:

1. Doing your research up front
2. Listening to the advice of other students and teachers
3. Observing lectures before registration

But always work with your instructors if you cannot, by:

1. Getting interested in their subject
2. Learning their style in the classroom
3. Knowing about their likes and dislikes

---

3. Never Miss a Class
(But always make up the work if it cannot be helped)

French dramatist Philippe Néricault Destouches said, "Those not present are always wrong." Destouches knew what he was talking about. Those not present when their teacher gives a lecture are always wrong, and that is why you should never miss a class—*never*!

The reason I say "never miss a class" is because most of the test questions will come from material that your teachers present in class. It is almost like a code of ethics with most teachers: They think it is unfair to test students on material that was not covered, or at least mentioned, in class. During every class, your teachers will present information that they think is important for you to understand the subject. Teachers bring all of their knowledge into the classroom and present it in a manner that they think is easiest for you to understand. They are more interested in what you know than what you do not know. If you can show your teachers that you have understood everything they have presented in class, then you are well on your way to earning an A in the course.

When you miss a class, you are running a big risk. Teachers may think that you are not interested in the subject and that you do not care to hear what they have to say. Moreover, there may be questions on the next test that are related to the material covered in class when you were absent. If you are taking an essay test with three or four questions and you do not know the answer to one of them, you might end up with a B or C on the test, even if you know the answers to all of the other questions. Can you afford to take that risk?

When I say "never miss a class," I am also saying "never miss *any part of* a class." Teachers communicate much of the important information at the beginning and end of a class. They usually use the first five minutes of a class to summarize important information from the previous class, or to make an important announcement such as the date of an upcoming test. They often use the last five minutes to summarize the content of the present class, or to make an assignment for the next class. If you arrive to class a few minutes late, or leave a few minutes early, you may miss part of a discussion by your teacher that is important. The part you miss may show up later as a question on a test. It is foolish to put yourself at a disadvantage with classmates who are there to hear the information.

The times when you arrive at and depart from class, as well as how you conduct yourself when you are there, create a definite impression in your teachers' mind. If you want to create a good impression, arrive at class on time, do not make any noise, be serious and interested in the subject, work very hard, and leave the class in a polite manner. If you start packing up your books five minutes ahead of time to beat your classmates out the door, this may create a disturbance and disrupt the message the teacher is trying to convey. By practicing good manners in the classroom, you will create a favorable impression. And a favorable impression may be the difference between receiving an A or a B in the course, especially if you are on the borderline. As I noted earlier, once you have made a bad impression, it is difficult to convert it into a good one.

A common mistake made by many students is to think that they can miss a class and make up for it by going over the reading assignments more carefully. This is a mistake because most teachers use more than the reading assignments to put together their classroom presentations. Teachers often use information that they learned as students, and update it using more current information to account for things that happened since they left school. If the school purchases new books, teachers may update their lecture notes to include information from the new books, but it is unlikely that they would change their notes completely. The only way to be sure what the teacher presented in class is to never miss one. Do not try to second-guess the teacher, because you will often be wrong!

Even if your teachers developed their class lectures entirely from the reading assignments, you would still miss something significant by not being there to hear them. Attending class changes you in a significant way, often in a manner that is not readily apparent. When you go to class, your teachers introduce you to new ideas, and you may leave the classroom with a different view of the world than the one you entered with. You will continue to learn even after you have left the classroom, because your mind will be grappling with the things you learned that day, rolling them over and exploring their various ramifications. This process occurs even when you are doing everyday activities, such as getting dressed, eating, walking to class, or talking with friends. You may find your mind silently going over facts you learned that day, or problems that you could not solve, trying to make sense out of them. When you miss class, you have short-circuited the whole process.

There is an old Greek saying, attributed to the philosopher Heracleitus: "You can't step twice into the same river." Once the water has moved downstream, it is no longer the same river—it has changed. It is very similar with classes missed at school. Once you miss a class it is gone forever, lost and lamented.

The worst possible time to miss a class is near the end of the grading period, but that is when students are most likely to miss them. Students tend to cut class at this time because their schedules are very busy, and they are trying to study for tests coming up in all of their subjects. It is very important to attend the final classes in a course, because teachers often use them to review subjects covered earlier or to let students know what they will be tested on in the final exam. Some teachers even tell students the specific questions that will be included on the exam, or at least the possible range of questions.

Teachers often use the final classes for a general question-and-answer session, in which students can ask about any topic covered during the course. This is a time when you can resolve any of the issues that gave you difficulty in the course, or anything else you may have wondered about. Some of the questions students ask may turn up as actual questions on the final exam, so it is important that you be there to hear the questions as well as the teacher's answers. If you do not attend these sessions, you may be at a significant disadvantage with your classmates who did attend, especially if the test results will be graded on a curve.

If there is absolutely no way you can attend a class, then you should try to obtain the notes for that day to make up for the material that you missed. In some cases, teachers post an outline of their notes or presentations online, so you can access them by computer. If this is not the case, the best approach is to try to borrow the notes from your teacher. Your teacher's notes will include just about everything that was covered in the class that day, except possibly some questions raised by your classmates. However, many teachers are not willing to lend their notes to any student, regardless of the circumstances.

If you were unable to get the lecture notes from your teacher, then you should try to borrow the notes from one of the better students in class. If you have any doubts, you might ask your teacher about a good candidate who is bright and writes clearly. Be advised that the student who loans you the notes may have missed or misunderstood some of the material presented, which means that you will have the same difficulty. A good indication that another student was not focused in class is the evidence of several unrelated "doodles" imbedded in his or her notes.

Once you have the notes from either the teacher or another student, you should rewrite them into your own notebook. It is not enough merely to read and return them. By rewriting the notes, you will force yourself to go over the material slowly and study it. If you do not understand everything—and I mean *everything!*—that your teacher or another student has written, then ask them for an explanation. This will help you keep up as best as possible, but you should not make a habit of missing class.

One of my former teachers announced his policy about attending classes on the very first day: "There is only one excuse for missing a class, and that is a death in the family— *your own!*" Although the teacher's remark was half intended as a joke, it is not a bad policy to follow.

I took his words very seriously, and set an example when I was attending graduate school. During the entire time that I was working on my Ph.D. in economics, I never missed a single class, or even a portion of a class. There were plenty of times when I might have had a legitimate reason to miss class, or did not feel well, but I always resisted the temptation. On one occasion, I had the flu and a temperature of 104 degrees, but I showed up for class and did my best. You may regard this as total fanaticism, but I regarded it as my duty. You will be surprised at what you can do if you feel you have to do it!

RECAP

Never miss a class or be tardy because:

1. It creates a bad impression in your teacher's mind.
2. You will miss important information that cannot be recovered.
3. Most test questions come from material presented in class lectures.

But always make up the work if it cannot be helped.

---

4. Always Sit in the Front Row
(Or get as close to the front row as possible)

American poet Emily Dickinson knew the importance of being up front:

> *But, looking back—the First so seems*
> *To Comprehend the Whole—*
> *The Others look a needless Show—*
> *So I write—Poets—All—*

When you are sitting in the front row of the class, you are much more likely to "comprehend the whole" of your teacher's lecture.

By sitting in the front row, you are putting yourself in the best possible position to learn. You will be able to see what the teacher is writing on the blackboard and hear the lecture more clearly than if you were sitting farther back in the class. You will comprehend much more of the material because you will not be disturbed by other things going on in the classroom. For example, you will not see other students moving around or hear them talking to one another, which creates a distraction. In the front row, all you can see is the teacher and the blackboard, and you will absorb the nuance of every word and thought.

Another reason for sitting in the front row is that your instructor will get to know you and think of you as a serious student. When you are in the front row, the instructor is much more likely to recognize you and think of you as a person, rather than a name or a number on a piece of paper. Classes in high school are small enough so that teachers will quickly learn the names of all of their students. Classes in some universities are so large and impersonal that instructors never get a chance to meet many of the students. When an instructor sees a student sitting in the front row, there is a subtle communication that the student is serious and ready to learn. In one of my courses in graduate school, shortly after classes had begun, the professor said to me, "Oh, I know you, you're the student who always sits in the front row." He probably heard that from one of the other professors.

Most students prefer to sit in the middle or back of the class rather than the front row, and the reason why is very clear. When you sit in the front row you feel more vulnerable, *because you are more vulnerable*! You have less privacy in the front row, and the teacher is more likely to call on you to answer a question. They do not do it out of meanness or spite. They do it because when you are talking to people, particularly when speaking to them directly, it is a natural human instinct to turn to the person closest to you. No one wants to look stupid by not being able to answer a question, and that is why most students do not want to put themselves in this position. You have to be very attentive and alert when sitting in the front row, and that is precisely why you should sit there! You will get much more out of your teachers' lectures if you are awake and alive rather than drifting off in a daydream.

Sitting in the middle or back of the class creates many problems that prevent you from absorbing 100 percent of the material. Because you do have more privacy in the middle or back of the class, you are more likely to think or work on something unrelated to the instructor's lecture. You will be distracted by looking at the back of all of the people in front of you—distracted by their motions, distracted by their conversations, and distracted by their idiosyncrasies. The boys will be looking at the girls, the girls will be looking at the boys, and everyone concerned will be thinking less about the lecture.

As you sit farther back in a large classroom, the problems become more serious. You cannot hear the instructor as well, and sometimes the message gets garbled. Some students become so relaxed that they actually fall asleep in their seat. And when the instructor singles them out for this behavior, it is even more embarrassing than not being able to answer a question when sitting in the front row.

Another reason why sitting in the front row is wise is that time will pass more quickly. There is an old saying that "time flies when you are having fun." The phrase is most often used in a disparaging manner to say that time passes very slowly when you are bored or feeling tortured. But the statement is true! When you are sitting in the front row, you will be so absorbed in everything going on that time will pass very quickly. I remember in graduate school that it often felt as if the class was over soon after it had started. I was so engrossed in everything going on that I had completely lost track of time. I was not "spaced out," just "wired in" to everything the instructor was saying. When you get this involved, the entire learning process becomes more enjoyable.

There are certain things you can do to ensure yourself a front-row seat. The average class has twenty to thirty seats or more, so not everyone can sit in the front row—*but not everyone wants to sit in the front row!* At the beginning of the class, if the instructor asks students where they want to sit, volunteer to sit in the front row. Sometimes teachers assign seats arbitrarily, or even alphabetically. If you do not get a front-row seat, then politely ask your teacher if you can move up front to hear better. In many university classes, seating is on a first-come, first-served basis. In this setting, you will have your best chance at a front-row seat by arriving early. If you come late and cannot get a front-row seat, then do not despair; just take a seat as close to the front row as possible. I think you will find, in most cases, that things will work out your way.

Regardless of the truth of what I have said, getting students to sit in the front row is one of the most difficult tasks imaginable, and they will do almost anything to avoid it. I have been working with students for many years, and one of the most frequent statements I have heard from them goes something like this: "Dr. Green, I will do everything you tell me, but please do not make me sit in the front row. I just hate it!" And what I tell them in return is that sitting in the front row is one of the easiest and most important steps in my study system, and if they do not do it then they are not really following my study system and will not get the best results. Do not think for a minute that you can follow all of my other steps except this one, and still be a top student.

I am sure that you have heard the statement that humans typically use only a small portion of their mental capacity, but they can use more if they are in the right environment. The way to use more of your mental capacity is to concentrate more deeply, but this will only occur if there are no distractions. Sitting in the front row will enable you to concentrate more deeply and retain more, so you will be more likely to reach your full mental potential. If you want to "comprehend the whole" of your instructors' lessons, always sit in the front row.

RECAP

Always sit in the front row because:

1. The instructor will get to know you as a person.
2. You will hear the lecture and see the blackboard more clearly.
3. You will not be distracted by the behavior of others.
4. You have to be prepared to answer questions.

Or get as close to the front row as possible.

---

5. Always Complete Your Homework Assignments Before Class
(So you will understand lectures and be prepared for questions)

"Alas! all things come too late for those who wait," said James Huneker, the American music writer and critic who was best known for his commentary on Chopin. If you wait until after class to do your homework assignments, alas, it will be too late! You will not be able to understand everything that your teachers present in class, and you will find yourself falling behind in your work.

Homework assignments generally fall into two categories: written assignments and reading assignments. Written assignments provide your instructor with immediate feedback about how much work you have done and how well you have understood the assignment. Although reading assignments generally do not provide immediate feedback to your instructor, they are just as important as written assignments for understanding a subject. Reading assignments will determine how much of your instructor's lecture you understand, how well you will be able to organize the information, how well you will perform on tests, and ultimately, how well you will do in the course.

When you enroll in a class, your first assignment is to find out what is expected of you in the way of homework assignments. In the lower grade levels, many instructors write the assignments on the blackboard for the next day or even week, so you will know where the course is heading. At the higher grade levels, it is common practice for instructors to hand out a course outline, or syllabus, at the beginning of the course. This is useful because it enables you to see where the entire course is heading, and the amount of work that will be required of you in the form of various assignments,

tests, and papers, and when they are due. After reading the
outline, make sure that you know exactly what the teacher
wants you to do. If you have any questions, do not hesitate to
ask. If the teacher provides additional guidance, be sure to
write it down on the syllabus or in your notebook.

Reading Assignments

Most course outlines list all of the books or articles that you
are expected to read during the entire term, and how to locate them. Textbooks are particularly important because
your teacher or the education department thinks that they
have an advantage over other books on the subject in terms
of content and presentation. In all likelihood, these textbooks will provide a useful introduction to the subject and
complement the material that your instructor presents in
class. In addition, course outlines often list books that are
recommended. Your instructor probably listed these books
because they include information that is not covered, or not
covered well, in your textbooks. It is a good idea to obtain *all*
books that are listed in the course outline, whether they are
required or recommended, because this will give you the
fullest understanding of the subject. I also recommend that
you obtain any articles that are listed in the course outline,
which may be available through an Internet connection at
your school if they are located in a professional journal.

The cost of obtaining all of these books can be considerable. At the lower grade levels, at least in public school, required textbooks are furnished by the school free of charge. At
the higher grade levels, in college and graduate school, the
student has to purchase the books and the price is not low
because the people who run the bookstore know that they
have a captive audience. Cost notwithstanding, you should
purchase all of these books and retain them after the course

is over, for future reference. Of the various books on a subject, the textbooks you used are probably the ones you are most comfortable with and knowledgeable about. They may also be very useful when you are taking a course on the same subject at a higher level, and need a handy reference.

As you can tell from the title of this section, the recommended time to complete your reading assignments is *before* the next class in which they are due. If you obtain nothing else from this section but this one thought, then my efforts will have been worthwhile.

By completing your reading assignments before class, you will be more familiar with the material when the teacher presents it in class, enabling you to comprehend and retain more of it. When you know something about a subject ahead of time, your teacher's lectures will seem more interesting and exciting because you can relate to them. This will make you a more active listener in class. It is always easier to understand more about a subject when you hear it a second time, because you have already thought about the relevant questions and their answers from your first reading. This will help you to organize and digest the material when it is presented in class.

If you still have questions about a subject after your first reading, then the classroom is an excellent place to raise and discuss them. You can bring up your questions before, during, or after class, depending upon when the occasion seems appropriate or when the teacher prefers to address them. Do not be shy or afraid to raise your questions, for fear that they will be viewed as silly or stupid. Most teachers like to entertain questions, because they demonstrate that students have been thinking about a subject. Moreover, if you have done your reading ahead of time, you should be able to answer many of the questions that the teacher raises in class. This will demonstrate that you are a serious and intelligent student, and that you have prepared for class. Few things impress a teacher more.

It is important for students to understand that they are doing their readings for a purpose, and that purpose is to understand the subject. If a subject is difficult and you did not fully understand it from your first reading, then go back and read it again if you have time. If you do this, however, it is still important to complete the reading assignment *before* attending the next class in which the teacher will discuss the subject, for all of the reasons mentioned earlier. If you start doing your readings after class, you will quickly fall behind in your studies, and you will not get the opportunity to discuss the subject in class. You may want to review the material briefly before a test, but the main reason for doing the reading assignments is to understand more of what the teacher presents in class.

In my many years as a student, I have seen other students make an absolute fetish out of doing their reading assignments. Some mark up their textbooks so badly that they can barely understand what the author has written. They highlight in various shades of felt-tipped pen or underline with pencil or pen, passages that they plan to read several times before taking a test. The ones who do this are the same ones who attend class irregularly or take sparse notes when they are there. Who knows if they have marked the relevant passages? In the first place, you should not be marking up any books that do not belong to you, because it is likely that you will have to pay for them later. In the second place, you should not be marking up your own books so badly that you will be unable to read them again. A few short, inconspicuous notes in a book are fine, but you may want to write more lengthy notes on a separate piece of paper. The important point is that you will likely be tested on how much material you understand, not how much you have memorized.

Do not think for a minute that you can take shortcuts around doing your reading assignments and still be a top student. Some students think that they can skip doing the reading assignments altogether, and rely instead on what the teacher says in class. The fallacy of this approach is that you need to do the reading assignments to gain a full understanding of what the teacher presents in class. Besides, there is usually much more to a subject than what the teacher discusses in class. Your teacher will not have time to discuss everything about a subject in class, only the more significant aspects. The readings may contain some interesting material or perspectives that you need to know to master the subject fully. The only way to get all of the information is to do all of the readings.

Written Assignments

Most of the subjects that you take in school will have written homework assignments, although there are some exceptions. Most mathematics and science courses require written assignments such as solving problems. It is the nature of these disciplines that you learn by doing, and you cannot go forward to the next step until you have mastered the previous one. Written assignments enable you to continue learning at home, and provide a good indication to your instructor of the rate at which you are progressing. Written assignments may be less frequent in English and social studies, but they still come at periodic intervals and are often more important in terms of their point value. I have had some courses in college in which there were no written homework assignments, but they were a rarity.

It is important for you to understand that watching your teacher solve problems on the board in class will not necessarily teach *you* how to solve them. As renowned Irish author George Bernard Shaw said, "If you teach a man anything, he will never learn." We learn by doing, so you need to roll up your sleeves and make some mistakes on your own by trying to solve the problems. Your goal should be to make the mistakes beforehand, such as when you are working on a homework assignment, so you will not make the same mistakes on a test.

Most teachers collect homework assignments, grade them, and then return them to students so they can see where they went wrong. It is imperative that you do these assignments and turn them in on time, both to let your teacher know that you are doing the work, and to enable yourself to progress at the proper pace. If you do not complete your homework assignments on time, you may find yourself falling behind, and recovery will be that much more difficult. It is always wise to turn in your homework assignments, even if they are late and there is a significant reduction in the point score, because homework assignments can be a significant part of your final grade. And do not forget to review your homework assignments when they are returned, so you will not repeat the same mistakes again.

Summary

It is very important for you to have the proper attitude about homework assignments. They are not something that teachers hand out to punish students; they are there to help you learn more about the subject. Once you understand this, it should be easier for you to approach your homework assignments with energy and enthusiasm rather than disdain.

If you are working on a homework assignment and come across something that you do not understand, then you should ask your teacher for an explanation. When I was in school I had to wait until the next class, but in today's world you are likely to send the teacher an e-mail ahead of time.

Asking questions shows your teachers that you are trying to learn the subject, which is why they assigned the homework in the first place. Just be sure not to overuse the privilege or you may be viewed as a pest. It is important for you to learn the answers to your questions beforehand, because problems similar to the homework may show up on the next test.

I have some tips that will help you to complete your homework assignments more efficiently and effectively. As soon as you get home from school or college, start thinking about the homework assignments that are due before each of your next classes. It might help to write down all of the assignments on a piece of paper, so you will be able to see the full extent of what is required. Then think about the order in which you will do them, and how much time will be required to complete each one. Sometimes this approach will help you get started, and the sooner you start, the quicker you will be done! I will have many more tips on homework assignments in the next chapter.

RECAP

Always complete your homework assignments before class, so you will:

1. Get full credit for doing the homework.
2. Be prepared for the next class.
3. Understand more of your teacher's lecture.
4. Ask and answer good questions in class.

Turn in your homework on time to earn the maximum points, but always turn it in even if late to salvage what you can.

---

6. Take Extensive Notes in Class
(So you will become an active listener
and retain more information)

In *Henry IV,* William Shakespeare wrote, "It is the disease of not listening, the malady of not marking, that I am troubled withal." What was true in sixteenth-century England is still true today. You must listen carefully to your instructors during lecture, and take extensive notes on what they say, if you have any hope of becoming a straight-A student.

Taking good notes is important at all levels of education. If you go into just about any college class, you will see most if not all of the students busily taking notes. They have learned that taking good notes is one of the keys to doing well in their courses. If you go into just about any class of younger students in high school, you will see few if any of them taking notes. Younger students have not learned the importance of taking notes, and probably many of them do not know how to take them.

Taking good notes is probably the most important step in my entire study system. You must listen carefully to your teachers during lectures to understand everything they say. Then you should try to capture everything important that they say in your notes, because you may be tested on this material. To do this, you must listen carefully, concentrate deeply, and then have a good system for writing down the important information so it will be part of your permanent record. If you obtain little or nothing from your teachers' lectures, then you should not expect to receive good grades in their courses. As noted earlier, most of the questions on tests come from the material that teachers cover in class. The purpose of this section is to show you how to become an active listener and an accomplished note taker.

How to Become a Good Listener

Most people, if asked, would probably say that they are good listeners, when in fact they may be poor listeners. The distinguishing quality of poor listeners is that they hear only what they want to hear, rather than what is being said. They may be suffering from any number of factors that keep them from being good listeners. For example, they may not be interested in the subject of the lecture, may not like their instructor, may be bothered by noise in the classroom or the behavior of other students, and may be affected by a number of other factors that inhibit concentration. You must be able to overcome all of these problems if you are to become an effective listener.

If you have been following all of the other steps in this chapter, such as sitting in the front row and doing your homework assignments before class, then you are already on your way to becoming an effective listener. More, however, is required.

To be a good listener, you have to be a good follower. Unlike reading, writing, and thinking, in which you have complete control, listening involves the presence of another person, in this case, your instructor. To be a good listener, you need to concentrate deeply on what your instructor is saying, and avoid drifting off on tangents. This is more difficult than it sounds, because you can think several times faster than your instructor can speak. Use this extra time to your advantage to think about what your instructor has said, record it into your notes, and anticipate his or her next thought. Do not spend too much time "thinking around the thought," because you will be more likely to drift off and miss your instructor's next thought. If your teacher says something intriguing, postpone thinking deeply about it at this point. There is plenty of time after class to think deep thoughts. The best approach is to temporarily accept what has been said, and be a good follower.

Please understand that I am not expecting you to blindly accept everything your teacher says, as if it were a pronouncement made ex cathedra (an incontestable statement from a supreme religious authority). Teachers are not perfect, and they make their share of mistakes, too. So, if your teacher says something that you do not understand, or that does not sound quite right, then by all means question it.

Always try to ask your questions in an intelligent manner. Ask questions if you really need assistance, but do not be in such a hurry that you interrupt your teacher or disrupt the class. When the time seems appropriate, raise your hand and wait patiently for the teacher to respond. If the teacher sees your hand and you do not get a response after a reasonable amount of time, it may be best to postpone your question until later. The best questions not only provide the answer you were seeking, but also teach the rest of the class something important about the subject. Unfortunately, it is sometimes difficult to know which category questions fall into until after you have asked them. The important point is to ask questions that are worthy of consideration, and not merely because you want to be heard.

Active listeners are very alert during lectures, because they know that they may have only once chance to understand their teacher's message. Listening is very different than reading a book, because you can go over passages in a book several times until you fully understand them. Listening does not provide that luxury, unless you are willing to ask many more questions than you should be asking. You must always be very attentive during a lecture, because you run the risk of missing something important that may appear later on a test.

The best way to stay alert during a lecture is to use all of your senses to gather information. Your eyes should be moving back and forth between the blackboard and your notebook, your ears should be listening to the words spoken by your teacher, your mind should be working to understand and distill what is important, and your hands should be recording the important information in your notebook. Your mind and body should be working continually to understand the nuance of every important thought and idea expressed in the classroom, and to record it faithfully in your notebook. When you become this involved in the lecture, you are less likely to drift off in a daydream.

The way to be a good listener is to be a good note taker, and the way to be a good note taker is to be a good listener. In other words, the two go hand-in-hand. We will now concentrate on how to become a good note taker, so you can complete the rest of the formula.

How to Become a Good Note Taker

The first rule of being a good note taker is to bring all of the proper supplies to class. This means that you should have a well-organized notebook with plenty of paper, and also plenty of sharpened pencils, erasers, pens, and other supplies that will be needed (such as rulers, compasses, or other equipment suggested by your instructor). High school students often prefer loose-leaf notebooks, because they may have to turn in assignments done in class and return them later to their notebook. College students often prefer spiral notebooks with pages that do not come out, because rarely do they turn in assignments done in class. When I was in graduate school, I bought separate spiral notebooks for each class, because I knew I would be taking extensive notes. I also preferred to take my notes in pencil rather than pen, so I could neatly erase and rewrite any mistakes made by the teacher or myself. Notes can become quite sloppy and difficult to read if you have to cross through numerous passages written in ink, and then rewrite them. I always used mechanical pencils for taking notes, because they eliminate the need for sharpening.

If you prefer to type your notes in class on a laptop computer, then that is acceptable, but I caution you to think about several factors before you make the decision. First of all, you had better be an accomplished typist, or you will find yourself quickly falling behind. Second, in some classes it will be difficult to take notes on a laptop computer, especially if there are complicated formulas such as those that often appear in mathematics and science classes. Third, think about what you will do if the battery dies on you, or if you somehow lose your work from the hard drive. For my taste, it is far too risky to take notes in class using a laptop computer.

The best way to capture everything of importance presented by the instructor is to take extensive, detailed notes by hand. You should be writing almost continually to record everything important that your teachers say in class. Forget about recording the small stuff, such as informal discussion, jokes, and other trivial matters. Try to write down your teacher's words and thoughts exactly as expressed, rather than translating them into your own words at this point— there is plenty of time for that later. If you get too involved in translating the teacher's words and thoughts into your own, you may miss his or her next thought.

When you use your notes to study for a test, you will quickly realize that they are only as good as the information that went into them. Therefore, you need to be very careful in what you write when taking notes. Be sure to copy *everything* into your notes that the teacher presents, such as graphs, charts, and tables. If the teacher uses a PowerPoint presentation projected onto a screen during the lecture, it may not be necessary to copy everything into your own notes, especially if these presentations are made available before class. If this is the case, be sure to print out a copy and bring it with you to class. You can then enter additional notes directly onto this copy. If your teacher tells you to organize all of the information in an outline, and actually writes one on the blackboard, be sure to include the outline in your notes. Do not become so concerned, however, about creating your own outline that you miss what the teacher is saying.

It is virtually impossible to write down every word that your teacher says in class, unless you know shorthand and write very fast. Therefore, I recommend that you use some different approaches that will enable you to write more quickly and still capture the essence of your teacher's thoughts.

One approach is to use abbreviations in your notes, and expand them later on. There are standard abbreviations that mean just about the same thing to everyone. For example, you can use letters and symbols to abbreviate words and phrases, such as "for example" (e.g.), "equals" (=), "does not equal" (≠), "and" (&), "with" (w/), and "without" (w/o). You can also use nonstandard abbreviations of your own creation, such as using the first few or last few letters in the word, leaving out selected vowels, and using contractions where possible. For example, you might use the abbreviation "gov't" for the word "government." Just be sure to use the same abbreviations for words consistently so you will be able to decipher them later on.

Another approach that will speed up your note-taking is to use shortened sentences rather than complete sentences. For example, when writing your notes you might leave out certain parts of speech such as prepositions and conjunctions that are not absolutely necessary to understand an idea. You need to be careful, however, not to leave out so many words that the thought is changed or it becomes impossible to understand what your shortened sentence means. The idea is to do as little writing as possible and still capture all of the essential facts, thoughts, and principles expressed by your teacher.

I also recommend that you leave plenty of white space on the page when taking notes. This will serve two important purposes. Your teacher may come back to the same subject during the lecture and provide additional information, which you will want to include in the correct location. Or you may want to go back later and supplement your notes with additional information, either in the form of spelling out some of the abbreviations or including thoughts of your own. Just be sure to develop an approach that enables you to distinguish between additional information supplied by the teacher as opposed to yourself.

Now that you will be taking extensive notes during lectures, you will need a good system to organize them. Start off by always writing down the date of the lecture and lecture number at the top of the first page before you begin to take notes. Number the pages starting with one and continue in sequence for each subsequent lecture. This is absolutely essential if you are using a loose-leaf notebook, so you can put pages back into their proper location should you need to remove them. It is also extremely useful if you are using a spiral notebook, because it will help you locate information quickly and easily. In your notebook, you should also write down all of your homework assignments, what they involve, and when they are due. Do this even if the homework assignments are listed in the course syllabus, so you will not forget them.

It is also to your advantage to keep a very neat notebook. If you are using a loose-leaf notebook, be sure to include labeled dividers that separate the pages for each of the subjects you are studying. It can become very disconcerting if pages from different subjects become mixed together. Also, clean and rearrange your notebook at regular intervals, so it does not become too thick and awkward. If you are using a spiral-bound notebook, do not include extraneous pages or materials that will clutter up your notes. Also be sure that notes include only essential information from lectures. Doodles or other drawings are an indication that your mind was straying from the subject, and they will be a distraction if you have to look at them later on when studying for a test.

As you take your notes during class, you should be looking out for potential exam questions. Teachers give hints all of the time, and sometimes repeat them several times over. If you are very alert, you may notice a change in your teachers' voice or movements that indicate they think a certain fact, event, or idea is particularly important. When teachers get very excited about a particular subject, there is a good chance that it might show up on a test. Some teachers may come right out during class and say that particular subjects would make good test questions. When they do this, be sure to record the information in your notes and mark it with an asterisk. If you can figure out the likely test questions before the exam, you will have a significant advantage over your classmates. You will have time to collect your thoughts and prepare a good answer before taking the test.

Teachers have different styles of presenting information in class, and, as a student, you should be able to recognize them. Some teachers use a PowerPoint presentation with an outline of their lecture notes. Others hand out a paper copy of an outline, or write one on the blackboard, listing what they plan to cover in class that day. Some teachers number their points, and go over them several times for emphasis, whereas others expect students to do most of the work. Still others hand out written summaries of the material they have covered in class, to provide a handy reference for students. If you can recognize your teachers' styles, you will get more out of their classes because you will know what to expect.

As a serious student, you should recognize that it takes a lot of energy and effort to learn. When taking detailed notes, your mind and body will be working almost every second that you are in class. As you become more involved in the learning process, you will become less aware of all of the work you are doing and time will pass very quickly. After perfecting your note-taking method, you will become more excited as you learn more about a subject. The entire learning experience will become more fun, and you will begin to look forward to your next classes to see how the story continues. You will enjoy being several steps ahead of your classmates, and sometimes, even a few steps ahead of your teachers.

You should not look for an easy way out to avoid all of the work that it takes to become a good student. For example, do not think that because the teacher uses a PowerPoint presentation that you will not have to take any notes in class. Do not think that you can use a tape recorder to skip taking any notes in class. In either case, you will be less likely to listen to your teacher in class, because you will know that you can look at the PowerPoint presentation or listen to the tape recorder later on. But it will not be the same, and something will be lost. For example, what are you going to do if you are listening to the tape recorder and the teacher is pointing to something on a blackboard that you cannot see? You will always understand and remember more of what your teacher says about a subject if you take notes immediately after hearing it.

There is one last, but very important, point that you need to understand: *Nothing that happens in class eliminates the need to take good notes.* Even if you understand everything that your teacher says in class, you will still have to take good notes because there is no guarantee that you will remember it later on. The only way to be certain that you will understand and retain the information is to take careful, detailed notes. This may be a lot of hard work, but as Thomas Edison said, "There is no substitute for hard work."

RECAP

Always take extensive notes in class, and to ensure that they are good notes:

1. Bring the proper supplies to class.
2. Be an active listener and follower.
3. Take notes on everything of importance.
4. Use abbreviations liberally in your notes.
5. Look for potential exam questions during lecture.

---

7. Review (or Rewrite) Your Lecture Notes Before the Next Class
(To get everything in order, and start studying for the next test)

"In this world second thoughts, it seems, are best," said Euripides, an ancient Greek dramatist who produced works of tragedy. In the academic world, second thoughts are also best, or you may experience your own personal tragedy of not mastering what your teacher has presented in class.

To understand everything that your teacher presents in class, not only do you have to take good notes, you also have to make sure that you know what is in them and correct any errors or fill in any gaps. For students in high school, my advice is to *review* the lecture notes and make any corrections before the next class. For students in college and graduate school, my advice is to *rewrite* or *type* the lecture notes and make any corrections before the next class. The reasons why I make a distinction between the different educational levels will become apparent in the following sections. Whether you are a high school student or an undergraduate or graduate student in college, the important point is that you need to master what your teacher presents in class, and going over your notes is the only way to do it. And doing it *before* the next class will enable you to learn at the same rate that your teacher presents the material, and begin your preparation for the next test ahead of time.

High School

Students in high school should *review,* but not rewrite, their lecture notes before the next class so they will have enough time to get everything done. In high school, students typically have classes in their various subjects every day, so they would not have time to rewrite all of their notes. They would spend so much time rewriting their notes that they would not have time to complete all of their reading and written assignments, and would quickly find themselves falling behind. That is why I tell high school students to *review and correct* their notes rather than rewrite them.

Shortly after attending a class, find a spot where you can really concentrate on what you have written in your notes. The reason I say *shortly* is because the sooner you sit down to review your notes, the fresher the information will be in your mind. As you review your notes, you should be rethinking and correcting the material that your teacher presented in class. If there are any abbreviations in your notes, you should be expanding them with complete words, sentences, and thoughts. As part of the process, you should be correcting anything in your notes that is incomplete or inconsistent, whether it came from your teacher or yourself.

Many students find it helpful to add an outline to their notes, to provide more structure to the content. I am not suggesting that you rearrange or reorder what your teacher presented in class, only that you add headings that outline the structure of your teacher's message. As you do this, make sure that you can distinguish major points, minor points, and supporting details. An outline makes it easier to understand the overall content of the lecture and where it is heading.

Some students also find it helpful to add their own thoughts and comments to the notes based on the teacher's lecture. This will make it easier for you to understand the material presented, and also helps you to think of a response if you are asked to express an opinion about a subject on a test. If you add comments and thoughts, just make sure that you can separate your own from those of your teachers. If you left plenty of white space on the page when taking your original notes, as I recommended in the previous section, this process will be greatly facilitated and your notes will not look cramped.

As you review and correct your notes, make sure that you really understand what you have written. In an earlier chapter I talked about the importance of being an active reader, so you should use these same skills to become an active reviewer. Make sure that you understand the main thrust of your teacher's message, be able to separate major points from minor points, and understand how each lecture complements and extends what was presented in earlier lectures. Ask numerous questions, particularly those of a critical nature that question the truth and accuracy of the material presented. Most important, ask questions about the meaning and importance of your teacher's statements, and think about which of them might be good test questions. As Albert Einstein, the world's most famous physicist, advised, "Learn from yesterday, live for today, hope for tomorrow. The important thing is not to stop questioning."

If you come across something in your notes that you just cannot figure out on your own, then make a point to ask your teacher about it before or during the next class, preferably before. You might be able to visit your teacher at the end of the class, after school ends that day, or before school begins the next day, to get an answer to a question or problem that is particularly difficult. By asking these questions, you will be able to keep up with your teachers' lessons, and they will know that you are a serious student who really wants to learn. This could be very significant if a teacher grades classroom participation.

There are two reasons why you should review your notes *before* the next class. First, by reviewing your notes, correcting them, and filling them in, you will be reinforcing what you have already learned. Second, and most important, you will already have started studying for the next test. You can never begin studying too soon for a test! Most students complain that they never have enough time to study for a test, and it is usually because they did not start soon enough. By starting immediately, you will be that much further ahead when you actually do sit down to study for the test.

College and Graduate School

Students in college, at both the undergraduate and graduate levels, should *rewrite* or *type* their lecture notes entirely before the next class to make sure they have mastered everything that the professor has presented in class. In college or graduate school, students typically have class every other day, or once or twice a week, so there is ample time to rewrite or type lecture notes before the next class and not fall behind. The reason why it is so important to rewrite or type lecture notes at the college and graduate level is that the material is much more difficult, and exam questions are more likely to come from the material your instructor presents in class. Remember, your professors "profess" a subject, and what this means is that they have a unique or expert way of understanding and presenting the subject. Your task is to show them that you can do the same!

When I was in graduate school, I always kept two sets of notebooks to record lectures for every class. Each was in the form of a permanently bound spiral notebook, in which the pages could not be removed. I used the first set of notebooks to take my lecture notes in pencil in each class. I would then rewrite my lecture notes in longhand, using a pen, into the second set of notebooks, before attending the next class. These permanent notes never left my room because I felt that I could not afford to lose them, given their importance in preparing for tests. By following this approach, you will also have a backup set of notes should you lose one of the notebooks that you normally carry to class.

In today's world, you may choose instead to type your lecture notes before the next class. This may enable you to complete the process more quickly, and the notes will be easier to read when you review them later in preparation for a test. You will also have a way to store your permanent set of notes on the computer, but just be sure that you have a backup in case your hard drive crashes. Be advised, however, that when you type your notes on the computer, in some classes you will want to leave plenty of white space on the page to write in complicated formulas or graphs that would be simply too burdensome—or nearly impossible!—to type. Whether to rewrite your lecture notes in longhand or type them is a choice that I leave up to you. Select the approach that works the best for *you*!

Shortly after a class is over, pick a good spot to rewrite or type your lecture notes. As you do this, basically you will be re-thinking the material that your professor presented in class. You will be translating your abbreviated set of lecture notes into complete thoughts and sentences. You will also be resolving any inconsistencies or incomplete thoughts raised during the lecture. During the rewriting or typing phase, make sure that you can distinguish major from minor points, and orga-nize your thoughts into outline form if this helps. As before, I am not suggesting that you rearrange the lecture material dur-ing rewriting or typing, but merely that you add some head-ings and outline the overall framework of the lecture. The advice that I provided earlier about adding your own thoughts to the lecture notes also applies here, because this can be very helpful if you are asked to express an opinion about a sub-ject on a test. It is important to have a clear indication of the thoughts that are your own as opposed to the teacher's.

The advice that I gave earlier about really understand-ing what you are rewriting (or perhaps typing) also applies here. When deciding what to rewrite or type, be an active reader and ask very probing questions about the meaning and importance of your professor's statements, and critique their truth and accuracy. Understand how each lecture con-tributes to a continuing theme, and think about the types of questions that your professor would likely ask on a test. Write or type these questions into your notes so you will not forget them later on. Because material at the undergraduate or graduate level can be very complex and technical, you may need to consult your textbook to obtain a full and accu-rate description of a subject, particularly if your professor has not provided one in class.

If your rewritten or typed lecture notes still contain in-consistencies, then you should try to get them resolved by con-tacting the professor as soon as possible, preferably *before* the next class. Your task may be more difficult than for a high school student, because you may need to make an appointment with your professor during his or her office hours if a personal visit is needed to resolve a particularly troublesome problem. If your question seems straightforward, you may be able to obtain an answer by sending an e-mail. You need to be careful, however, because if you send too many e-mails you may be viewed as a pest. Frequent contact is valuable because it ensures that you and the professor are on the same wavelength. It also sends an important signal to the professor that you are a serious student who is actively engaged in the learning process. Just be judicious in how you go about it!

The most effective way to master ideas is to rewrite or type them, because this forces you to rethink them in a very deliberate manner. During rewriting or typing, your mind becomes more familiar with the material and you begin to internalize it. Your rewritten or typed notes will be expressed in a form that is most understandable to *your* mind. This will make it much easier to review your notes later on when studying for a test, because you will not need to relearn the material. Thoughts developed in this manner have much greater residual power than those not developed with deep thought. I can still remember many of the things that I learned years ago in school. This is an important quality, because Albert Einstein also said, "Education is what remains after one has forgotten everything he learned in school." You should not want to forget!

I cannot emphasize strongly enough why it is essential to rewrite or type lecture notes as soon as possible. By rewriting or typing your lecture notes *before* the next class, your grasp of the material will be at its strongest, because the information is still fresh in your mind. If you wait a long time before rewriting or typing, you may have difficulty reconstructing what the professor said in class, to be able to fill in the missing pieces. Moreover, as I emphasized earlier, the most important reason for preparing your lecture notes *before* the next class is that you have already started to study for the next exam. You cannot begin too soon in studying for a test!

Although my recommendation to rewrite or type lecture notes may be controversial, I think it is one of the most important steps in my entire study system, particularly for college and graduate students. Some other study guides advise students not to rewrite or type notes, referring to it as a superstitious, mindless, and time-consuming activity. The typical approach that these study guides recommend is to outline the professor's presentation during lecture, translating his or her thoughts into your own words. They then advise the student to reread the lecture notes shortly after class, and supplement them with additional information as necessary. I have found it more effective to faithfully record what the professor says in class, and then rewrite it into a separate set of lecture notes after class, with supplementation as necessary. All I can tell you is that I have tried it both ways, and I think that my approach works best. As the acid test, you can compare my grades with those of other authors who espouse the alternative view!

Potential controversy aside, I always encounter much difficulty when trying to convince college students of the importance of rewriting or typing their lecture notes. College students are notorious procrastinators. Even though rewriting or typing lecture notes is an easy, straightforward task, many students will make a chore out of it. They will view it as a time-consuming and laborious activity, or put off doing it altogether. They may think that writing their notes once during the lecture is sufficient to master the material. In all likelihood, they will put off looking at their lecture notes until right before a test, and then they will be surprised that much of what they have written does not make any sense.

General Recommendation

My view is that time spent either reviewing (or rewriting or typing) your lecture notes, as appropriate to your level in school, is time well spent. It may take you a little more time in the short run to prepare your lecture notes in this manner, but it should take you less time in the long run when you review them for a test. Your understanding will be much greater because you have already mastered the material, and put it into a form you can completely understand, so the review will be much easier and more comfortable. You will also have more confidence when you take a test, because you are just reviewing what you already know.

I recognize that it will take some time and discipline for you to complete all of your work. You will need to review (or rewrite or type) your lecture notes before the next class, and still complete all of your reading and writing assignments on time. To get everything done on time, you will need to spend your time wisely. After a while you will probably develop a system of what to study when. In a later chapter, I will be providing some study tips to help you organize your time. It is possible to get everything done on time, and still have plenty of time left over to do all of the other things that you want to do with your life.

If you really want to become a straight-A student, then you need to follow every single step in my study system. If you skip just one of my study steps, then you are not really following my system. Reviewing (or rewriting or typing) lecture notes before the next class is absolutely essential!

Here is some evidence that supports my argument. Research has shown that average people remember only about 20 percent of what they have read, 40 percent if they hear it after they have read it, and 60 percent if they also write it. Thus, even if you do all your readings, go to every class and listen very carefully, and take detailed notes, you will only know enough to earn a bare passing grade (60 percent is a D-minus in most grading systems) if you do nothing else. So consider this: By reviewing (or rewriting or typing) your lecture notes, you will increase your mastery of the subject matter and you will understand and remember much more than 60 percent.

The remaining sections and chapters in this book will show you how to increase your understanding of a subject as close to the 100 percent mark as possible.

RECAP

Review your lecture notes if you are a high school student, and rewrite or type them if you are an undergraduate or graduate student in college.

In both cases, do it *before* the next class!

To do this effectively:

1. Organize your notes so you can understand them.
2. Spell out the abbreviations and fill in any missing information.
3. Check with your teacher to clear up any inconsistencies.

Feel good about your situation, because you have already started studying for the next test!

---

8. Start Reviewing Your Lecture Notes and Reading Materials One Week Before a Test
(So you will be fully prepared to take it)

Scottish novelist Robert Louis Stevenson said, "Even if the doctor does not give you a year, even if he hesitates about a month, make one brave push and see what can be accomplished in a week." There is nothing particularly magical about one week, but the point is that you need to start studying early enough to do well on a test. As Stevenson said, you can accomplish a lot in just *one week!*

One of the main reasons that students do not do well on tests is that they do not allow themselves enough time to study. Many students think that they can wait until the last day before a test, and cram everything into their heads up to the last minute. By this time it is too late! You need to be fully prepared to do well on an exam, and a week normally provides ample time to get everything done. If your instructor does not give you this much time after announcing an exam, then you need to start studying as soon as possible.

You may not realize it, but you have already been studying for an exam much longer than a week if you have been following my study system up to this point. By doing your reading assignments before class, taking careful notes in class, and either reviewing or rewriting your lecture notes before the next class, you have mastered material as it was presented to you. This does not mean, however, that you are ready to sit down and take a test. After the passage of some time, the facts and ideas that you know begin to get a little hazy, even if they were very clear when you first learned them. They may still be in your memory, but the longer the time since your last test, the weaker your understanding is likely to be. That is why all students, no matter how attentively they have attended class, need to review their lecture notes and reading materials before taking a test if they are to do their best.

Most teachers announce the dates for their examinations well in advance to give students ample time to study for them. Many teachers, particularly those at the college and graduate levels, announce or hand out their examination schedule at the beginning of the semester or term. This enables students to prepare their schedule carefully, so they can get every-thing done even if they have several examinations from dif-ferent courses in the same time period. If your teacher has not announced or listed an examination schedule in advance, be sure to inquire about it—repeatedly, if necessary.

Some teachers like to preserve the element of surprise by giving unannounced "pop quizzes," to make sure that their students are keeping up with their studies. If you have to take a pop quiz, rest assured that you will be far better pre-pared than your fellow students if you have been following my study system, because you have been studying as you go.

To prepare for an announced exam, you will need to re-view your lecture notes and reading assignments since the last test. Let's look at each in turn.

Reviewing your lecture notes will help you be certain that you have mastered everything that your teacher has presented in class. The steps you have already followed with your lecture notes illustrate the "power of reinforcement." Because you have already been reviewing or rewriting your notes, making corrections and filling in missing informa-tion, your task will be that much easier. If you have rewrit-ten your notes, the information is in a form that is easiest for you to understand and all inconsistencies have been re-solved. The information is already ingrained in your mind, and all you need to do is review it sufficiently to make sure that you have command over it. Once you have command over the material, you will have command over the test.

Reviewing your reading materials will help you to be cer-tain that you have mastered all other assigned material, even if your teacher did not cover it in class. As noted earlier, your teacher probably assigned much of this material to give you a better understanding of what was presented in class, but there could be some additional material that may show up on a test. It will not be necessary for you to go back and reread everything, particularly if the reading assignments were very long. Sometimes you can get by if you make an outline of the key points in the readings. In many courses, such as English, social studies, mathematics, and science, you are asked to answer questions at the end of each reading assignment that test your knowledge. When preparing for a test, it may be sufficient to go back and read your answers to these questions, and perhaps glance through the chapter to remember what was in it. On the other hand, if your teacher tells you to reread a chapter in its entirety because it will be important on a test, then you had better do it.

It's as Easy as One, Two, Three . . .

As you can tell from the title of this section, you should start your review of these materials one week (if possible) in advance. Sometimes it is difficult to get started. If so, gather up your reviewed or rewritten lecture notes, any question or problem sets that you answered, and your books or articles that were reading assignments, and make a determination to sit down and get started. You should read over the lecture notes and question or problem sets, and briefly review (but not reread) the reading assignments. If you do not finish reviewing all of this material on the first day, then pick up where you left off on the second day. During this *first* reading, you should *not* try to memorize or relate the complicated material. That will come later. The purpose of this first reading is to go over everything to refresh your memory, and build up your confidence that you have a basic understanding of the material that will be covered on the test.

The best way to understand and master information is to reread it several times and think about it very deeply, and that is why you need to do a *second* review. After you have finished your first review, you should have several days left before the test. Take a short breather, and then begin your second review.

In this second review, you should concentrate mostly on your reviewed or rewritten lecture notes, but refer back to your question or problem sets and reading assignments as needed.

Your second review should be much more active than the first. Make sure that you understand important definitions, major and minor points, and the facts and details under these points. Sometimes the way to get command over the information is to recite the details during your review. If you have trouble remembering the details, try to relate them to something that you are already knowledgeable about. In fact, if you can relate the details to something that you have actually experienced, it may be even easier to remember them. Sometimes it is easier if you can remember just a few words that will trigger your memory so you can recall much more substance about a subject.

You should find your second review to be considerably easier than the first. You should start to anticipate the *sequence of ideas* as you turn the pages of your lecture notes, because the material is still fresh in your mind from the first review. You should start to feel that you are internalizing the information, so you can use it any way you want if you are tested on it. As you master the material, you should begin to feel more comfortable and your self-confidence should soar.

After finishing your second review, take a short breather and begin your *third* review. You should still have a few days left before the test. By this time, you should almost be able to anticipate the *content* of the next page in your lecture notes even before looking at it. Even more important, you should now be able to look at information in your lecture notes and reading materials and see the interrelationships between them. This is very important, because teachers like to ask questions on tests that require you to explain, relate, and compare information that comes from several different sections of your lecture notes or reading materials. Although you should be giving most of the emphasis to your lecture notes at this point, do not hesitate to refer back to your question or problem sets and reading materials, as needed, to tie everything together.

I recommend that you review your lecture notes *three* times to prepare adequately for a test, and refer to your other study materials as needed. I do not think it is necessary to do more than this, unless you find a subject to be particularly difficult. After a certain point, diminishing returns set in and you will not get as much benefit from additional reviews because you have already learned a substantial amount about the subject. On the other hand, if you do only one or two reviews, you may not have full mastery of the subject and you may do poorly on the test.

I have a favorite saying that comes from an old Elizabethan manuscript, which is particularly apropos here:

> *Multiplication is vexation,*
> *Division is as bad;*
> *The rule of three doth puzzle me,*
> *And practice drives me mad.*

Whether "the rule of three doth puzzle [you]," or "practice drives [you] mad," you need to face up to the fact that you should review your study materials three times before a test to get top marks. It is the best, if not only, way to do it!

I have some additional rules that will help you prepare for tests while you are reviewing your study materials:

Think About Potential Exam Questions

It is impossible to guess all of the questions that may appear on a test, because much of the obvious material is never tested. Nevertheless, guessing some of the questions is not as difficult as it may sound, because the information you learn in a subject can usually be grouped into major categories. After reviewing your study materials three times, these groupings should become obvious to you.

After these categories become obvious, make up some hypothetical test questions and see if you can answer them. It is not necessary to write anything down, but you should think about how to organize the information to write the best answer. Recite the answer to yourself, silently or out loud. By rehearsing in this manner, you will have a better understanding of the material and you will remember it for a longer period of time. This will also give you good experience in expressing yourself, which is what you will be asked to do on a test. This drill is very useful because it will help you prepare for the real test.

Rewrite Complicated Equations, Formulas, Charts, and Graphs

Some subjects, such as mathematics and science, require the use of a number of symbols, equations, formulas, charts, and graphs. Reviewing your study materials three times may not be enough to make you comfortable with the material. Sometimes the best way to get familiar with these expressions is to write them several times, so you will know them by heart. I think you will find that you can remember mathematical expressions much more readily if you write them down several times. This exercise is particularly useful for learning graphs, because it will enable you to remember the correct relationship for the various lines and the proper labels for the axes.

You can rewrite these expressions on a piece of paper, in your notebook, on the blackboard, or on anything else you choose. The approach I used was to write them directly into my finished set of lecture notes. I would write my permanent set of lecture notes on the right page, which left plenty of room on the left page to practice writing mathematical or scientific expressions, or to include additional notes. I could then compare my rewritten expressions with my lecture notes

on the opposite page to make sure that I had written everything down correctly. This exercise will give you excellent
practice in preparing for an exam. If you are still having difficulty remembering expressions, then you can write them
down on separate pieces of paper and glance at them periodically, right up to the day of the test, if necessary.

Pay Attention to Materials that Your Teacher Distributes in Class

Teachers sometimes hand out additional reading materials,
particularly if they did not have time to cover all of the information in class or if a subject is complicated. The mere
fact that a teacher has handed these additional materials
out should underscore to you how important they are in the
teacher's mind. You should treat these materials as if they
are just as important as the information that the teacher
covered in class. Review these materials carefully, and take
notes if that will help you understand them better. Make
sure that you understand any relationship between the materials the teacher hands out and the material covered in
class. This type of information has an uncanny tendency to
show up on tests, so it is wise to be prepared.

If your teacher announces that you will be tested on certain assigned readings, you should treat this material as if it
were presented in class. This does not mean that you should
take detailed notes on all of the readings, but you should
make sure that you have mastered the material. In most
cases, it will be sufficient to outline the relevant parts of the
readings, and review them along with your lecture notes
and other study materials.

Memorize Relevant Information if Necessary

In some courses in school you will need to remember certain
information, such as key dates, definitions, formulas, and

equations. The higher you go in school, there is usually less emphasis on memorizing and more emphasis on understanding. Some courses are exceptions, however, such as foreign languages and certain sciences, where memorization will be essential to succeed. In most cases, you will probably be able to remember what is needed from reviewing your lecture notes or completing your reading assignments. But sometimes more is needed. The big problem is that many students do not know the proper technique to memorize information. Many will stare at the words on a page for a lengthy period of time, hoping to absorb them through a process not unlike osmosis, and then they are frustrated when nothing happens.

I would like to suggest a more effective approach for memorizing information. Flash cards can be an invaluable tool. Write the information that you want to remember on three-by-five inch index cards. You can write the word or idea on the front of the index card, and the information that you want to remember on the back of the card. Then, when you have some spare time, you can glance at the front of the card and see if you can remember what is on the back of the card. After repeated efforts, the information will start to sink in. You can repeat this approach as often as needed, until everything becomes part of your memory.

Conduct Your Review in an Organized and Continuous Manner

The key to a successful study program is to begin your review well in advance, and to continue studying throughout the period leading up to an exam. It is best if you try to study at least something every day, or at least every other day, rather than putting aside your study materials for several days. This will enable you to get command of the material more quickly, because you will not need to go back and remember where you left off at the last review. The more time that elapses between reviews, the longer it will take you to get caught up. I know that studying continuously can be difficult, particularly if you are taking several courses or participating in extracurricular activities, but you just need to be diligent in the period before a test because so much is at stake. It might be a good idea to use a calendar during these study periods, so you can monitor how you are using your time.

Some study guides advise students to "think small," to study in short rather than long time periods when preparing for a test, but I disagree with this approach. You will find that you can accomplish much more if you study for several hours at a time rather than dividing your time into brief intervals. The reason that long study periods are more effective is that they give you time to understand the interrelationships between the various topics in a subject, which is the stuff that exams are made out of. My philosophy is to "think big," both in terms of completing as much work as possible when studying and getting the highest possible scores on exams.

Never Study Up to the Last Minute Before a Test
Studying up to the last minute before a test is a very disconcerting experience, because it gives you a rushed feeling and creates a mental impression that you are not fully prepared to take a test. It literally means that you have run out of time because you did not start studying early enough. As you can imagine, your self-confidence will be higher if you do not have to cram everything into your head in the final minutes preceding the test. A much better approach is to stop the day before, or at least a few hours before, a big test is scheduled. Besides, to do really well on a test, you need to be fully rested, calm, and mentally sharp. Rest is especially important, so you should get a good night's sleep before the day of the exam so you can perform up to your maximum potential.

Study Groups

I know that many students like to use study groups with their fellow students to prepare for a test, but you should approach them with caution. A study group is only as good as the caliber of people who comprise it. If you do get into a study group, make sure that you join with a group of students who are mentally sharp and have something to contribute rather than expecting you to do all of the work. And beware of students who think that they know more than they really do, because the misinformation they provide can be especially damaging.

I will confess to you that I *never* used study groups during the entire time I was in school, and, candidly, I guess I am too much of an individualist to even try one. I felt that I had a good study system that would enable me to understand the material, and that other students would not be able to contribute much beyond it. If there was something I did not understand, I could always go directly to the instructor for assistance. To me, studying is a solitary endeavor, not a social affair. One thing is for certain: Taking tests is a solitary endeavor because your fellow students will not be there to hold your hand and give you the answers; if they are, it is called cheating!

The important thing to understand is that if you want to do well on exams, you have to study for them. There is no other way around it. Do not think for a minute that you can walk into an exam without studying, and get lucky because the teacher will only ask questions on the subjects you are knowledgeable about. The whole purpose of an exam is to test what you know, and possibly what you do not know, and to do well consistently you need to be prepared for anything and everything!

RECAP

Start reviewing your lecture notes and reading materials *one week* before a test, so you will be fully prepared to take it. To do this effectively:

1. Review your lecture notes *three* times.
2. Refer to your question or problem sets and reading assignments as needed.
3. Think about potential exam questions and try to answer them.
4. Conduct your review in a continuous and organized manner.
5. Never study up to the last minute before a test.

You will do much better on a test if you are fully rested, so get a good night's sleep.

---

9. Be Testwise and Confident When Taking a Test
(Because these are the qualities that lead to success)

There is a verse for the devout in the English Book of Common Prayer that reads: "Examine me, O Lord, and prove me: try out my reins and my heart." Even though you will be going before a much lesser authority when you take a test, the need to be prepared is still present. Your instructor may not try out your reins [kidneys] and your heart, but you can be sure that he or she will try out your mind and your wits. Your chances of success will be much greater if you are testwise and confident.

The first and foremost principle of taking tests is that

you need to know what you are doing. Chapter 6 of part 2 was concerned with the basic skills of how to take different types of tests. The present chapter presumes that you have already learned these basic skills, and are ready to move on to some of the more advanced and esoteric aspects of taking tests, such as how to be testwise and confident. If you did not fully master the basic skills for taking tests from the earlier chapter, you should go back and read it again so you will be ready for the more advanced aspects in this chapter.

If you have been following the first eight steps of my study system, you should have complete mastery over the material, but the task now is to demonstrate this mastery to your instructor. If your instructor asks for a basic recitation of material on a test, your task is very straightforward. All you have to do is recite what you have already learned. It is unlikely, however, that your instructor will ask you to regurgitate the material verbatim on a test. The most effective tests ask you to use the information that you have learned to solve a problem that is new. This may require you to combine the information in ways that were not discussed by your instructor. This is similar to the way you will have to approach problems in the real world, because rarely will they fall into neat textbook examples. Tackling new problems is always a challenge, whether they are encountered inside or outside the classroom.

Instructors are particularly fond of asking you to use methods you have learned in the classroom to solve problems on tests. These methods are like a bag of tools available to a skilled craftsman. Like the craftsman, you will need to know which tools to use in solving particular problems, and demonstrate your skill in using them. This is particularly true in mathematics and the physical sciences, because you will have to use equations and formulas to solve problems. It is also true in the social sciences, because mathematics and graphical analysis are increasingly in vogue, particularly for the higher-level courses. Other disciplines require different sets of tools. On an examination, you need to demonstrate that you can use the tools of the trade like an accomplished journeyman, if not a master.

The first rule for success when taking an exam is that you need to have a completely open mind. Even though you may have thought beforehand about the questions likely to be asked on an examination, never try to force your answers into the exact mold you anticipated. Your instructor may be asking you to apply your knowledge in a different way from what was presented in class. The truly challenging tests ask you to move outside your normal way of thinking and be creative.

It is easier to be creative on a test than you might at first imagine, especially if you have been following my earlier steps. If you started studying for a test a week in advance, and reviewed your lecture notes three times along with other study materials, then you have loaded an enormous amount of information into your mind. Your mind will be working with all of this information in the days before the test, sometimes on a subconscious level, trying to make sense of the various facts, ideas, and relationships, and how they all fit together. This should put you in a creative mood when the day of the test arrives.

To get the most out of your creativity, you should go into an exam with the proper mental attitude and a high degree of self-confidence. Try to think of a test as an opportunity to show your instructor how much you have learned, not as an unpleasant hurdle that you are forced to leap over. If you have been following my study system faithfully, you should have peace of mind because your mind will be well organized. If you are confident, you are more likely to do well because you will have the right mental attitude. It is what is referred to as a "self-fulfilling prophecy"—if you think that you will do well on the test, then you probably will, and if you think that you will do poorly on the test, you probably will!

This notion may sound a little simplistic, but it operates in sports all of the time and also applies in the classroom. If you have played sports, I am sure that you have heard your coach talk about the importance of being confident during a game. Confidence helps athletes to perform at their highest level, and gain an advantage over their opponents. Taking a test is similar to playing a game, because you are competing against the teacher and other students in the classroom. The teacher is challenging you to answer a set of questions, and you are competing with other students to see how well you can do. In a sense, you are also competing with yourself, because you are trying to make your answer as good as possible to earn the highest score. As with an athletic competition, aim your sights high and try to reach the pinnacle!

At the opposite end of the spectrum of human emotions is fear, and the fear of taking tests is one of the most commonly encountered emotions. Some students experience fear and anxiety even at the thought of taking a test. They get nervous and worried about taking tests, and may even feel ill, because they are worried that they might fail. Then they start to fantasize about all of the terrible things that will happen to them if they do fail. They worry about the criticism and ridicule that they will get from parents, teachers, and possibly even other students.

One of the reasons students become so anxious about taking tests is that they think about what they have to lose if they do poorly. This is particularly true of students who have put a lot of time and effort into studying for a test, and want to be rewarded for their efforts. The very thought that they may do poorly on a test makes them nervous and anxious. This is very unfortunate, because sometimes they become so nervous and anxious that they cannot think clearly during the test, and thus bring about the very result that they hoped to avoid.

The main reason that students become frightened about tests is that they lack self-confidence. Students who have done poorly on tests in the past, as well as those who are not confident about the way they have studied for a test, will be the ones who are most frightened and nervous. If you have been following all of the steps in my study system, then you should be confident that you will do well on tests. As you put these methods into practice and experience success on examinations, you should become even more confident, because you will know that you have done everything possible to earn a high grade.

An important principle for students to understand is that the fear of failure is very different than the desire to succeed. It is very natural to get "psyched up" about a test in anticipation of what is to come. Strong emotions and a healthy flow of adrenaline can heighten your senses and sharpen your mental abilities, which will improve your performance on a test. It is similar to "getting up" for a big game in an athletic event, because of all of the excitement. This is a very different reaction, indeed, from fear.

If you have been afraid of taking tests in the past, then how should you go about getting rid of this fear? After all, it is very difficult to change our emotions immediately, like turning a light switch off and on. You may find it easier to diminish your fear if you have a better understanding of what tests are all about. Teachers design tests to measure your understanding about a subject, and to determine where you need to make improvement. Tests do not say anything about you as a person, or how smart you are, only how much you know about a subject at a given time. Sometimes tests are less threatening if you think about them in this manner. You should never think less of yourself as a person because you have done poorly on a test.

Think of tests as a learning tool for helping you and your

teacher measure your progress and improvement, and do not worry about making mistakes on them. As human beings, we are all going to make mistakes. No one is perfect. I have made plenty of mistakes on tests during my lifetime, and I am sure that you will make plenty, too. Your goal should be to make mistakes before you take an exam, learn from them, and avoid repeating them when you actually take the exam. This is easier said than done. As Søren Kierkegaard, the Danish existential philosopher, observed, "Life can only be understood backwards; but it must be lived forwards." By continually learning from your mistakes, however, you should make fewer of them in the future.

Most teachers review the correct answers when they return tests to their students, and this presents an opportunity for you to discover where you went wrong. You should be very attentive during these review sessions. If you have made mistakes on an exam, it is important for you to understand them so you will not make the same mistakes on the next exam, on the final, in the next course, or during the rest of your lifetime. Your first response to the discovery of a mistake should be open willingness to repair the damage and move forward. We gain real intelligence by learning from our mistakes, and set the stage for future growth.

Tests also enable you to gather valuable information about how teachers design them. Although teachers do not necessarily ask the same questions in all of their classes on a subject, and may change the questions from one year to the next, they often ask the same type of questions. You should try to learn something about the types of questions your teacher likes to ask, so you will be fully prepared when the next test is given.

After a teacher gives a test, you should be able to learn valuable information about his or her style in asking questions. This is similar to the way a master detective learns the behavior patterns of criminals by studying their MO (in

Latin, their modus operandi, or mode of operation) to antic-ipate their next move. After the first test, you should analyze the situation. Did the teacher give an objective test (true-false, multiple choice, or fill-in-the-blank), an essay test, or some other type of exam? What types of questions did your teacher ask? Were you asked to memorize facts, understand relationships between ideas, or solve complicated problems? Were the questions very broad, very narrow, or something in between? By understanding your teacher's MO, you will be better prepared for the next test or the final exam.

You will also have a better appreciation of tests if you un-derstand how teachers grade them. Most teachers give grades according to what is called the "normal distribution" in statis-tics. In other words, only a few students will get the highest grades, most will be in the middle, and only a few will fail. Al-though teachers sometimes proclaim that everyone can get an A or everyone can get an F, usually the school forces them to adhere to some type of distribution when giving grades. This means that you will have to compete vigorously with your fel-low students to get one of the few A's that will be awarded. You should not shy away from competition because it can actually be instrumental in raising your performance. In other words, competition in the classroom can be healthy, just as competi-tion in the economy encourages firms to become more efficient in producing better goods and services at lower prices.

When your teacher uses a distribution system to assign grades ("grades on a curve"), the grade you receive is not only a reflection of how well you did on the test, but how well your classmates performed. If there are a number of good students in your class, there will be a lot of competition for the top grades. On the other hand, if the other students in the class are not well prepared, it will be easier for you to come out on top.

Students are very aware of the effect that good students have on the grading distribution in a course, and whether a teacher will grade on a curve. When I was in graduate school studying economics, before every registration period one student would always ask me what courses I was taking the next semester. When I asked him why he wanted to know, he said, "If one student in the class gets 100 percent on a test then the teacher will know that he has done his job, and he may not grade on a curve. I don't want to be in the same classroom with *you!*" It was one of the nicest compliments I ever received.

Actually, the way most teachers assign grades on a test is even more complicated than I have described. The grade you receive may depend on the grade the teacher gave other students before getting to your test paper. This is particularly true on essay tests, in which the teacher needs to review several test papers to understand how well the class did on the exam, to set a standard for performance that is above, at, or below average. In such cases, it is difficult to say whether it is to your advantage to be at the front or rear of the pack, but this is not a matter in which you have any say.

The grade you receive on a test depends mainly on the factors that your teacher thinks is important. Some teachers put an emphasis on understanding ideas and presenting answers in an organized manner. Others put more emphasis on understanding the relationship between ideas and seeing the big picture. Some will put a lot of emphasis on grammar, spelling, and handwriting, whereas others will hold these qualities less dear. Still others may be influenced by how much they think you know, based on your classroom participation, and this factor may enter subtly in their grading of papers. The critical task is to find out as soon as possible what your teacher *thinks* is important, so you will know what to emphasize on tests.

You will be far better off, in both the short run and the long run, if you concentrate on learning a subject rather than worrying about your grade. In most cases, if you truly understand a subject, good grades usually follow. In some cases, however, you may have a good understanding of a subject, but still do poorly because things did not go right for you on a particular test. If you tried very hard to understand a subject, and put forth your best effort on a test, this by itself should give you some satisfaction—even if your grade was not as high as you had hoped. I am not recommending that you be satisfied with grades beneath your ability. You should always aim for the top, and strive to make the highest grade possible. What I am saying is that sometimes it takes time and practice to reach the very top. Keep following the strategies I have presented, and success will surely follow!

RECAP

To be testwise and confident when taking a test:

1. Believe in your ability to excel.
2. Keep an open mind.
3. Understand your teacher's MO (modus operandi).
4. Know how tests are graded.
5. Apply what you know.

Because these are the qualities that lead to success!

---

10. Show Your Instructor What You Have Learned on the Final Exam
(Because it is a big part of your final grade)

"Every advantage in the past is judged in the light of the final issue," said Athenian statesman Demosthenes. By the same token, every advantage—and disadvantage!—over the entire semester or year in school will be judged in the light of your performance on the final exam!

Many teachers give a final exam at the end of a semester or year to gauge how much students have learned about a subject. The final exam grade has a disproportionate effect on your overall grade in a course because it is the last exam given. In a sense, it tells your teacher what you are walking away with after completing the course. Some instructors in college will give students a grade in the course equal to the grade that they received on the final exam, regardless of past performance. It is something akin to the Christian ethic—you can repent at the last moment and still redeem yourself. Even in high school, a good grade on the final exam is likely to raise your overall grade significantly.

Before formulating your study plan for a final exam, you need to find out what material will be covered on it. Most instructors are very candid about the material that they will hold you responsible for on the final exam. If you have an instructor who has not been forthcoming, ask specifically if the final will cover material presented since the last exam or from the beginning of the entire course. Their answer to this question will determine how you should go about studying for the final exam.

The key issue in studying for a final exam is how much material you will need to review. If the final will only cover material presented since the last exam, then you should study for it as for any other test you took in the course. In other words, review your lecture notes and other study materials since the last exam, just as I have described in the earlier part of this chapter. If, on the other hand, the final exam will cover the entire semester or year, then you need to go back to the very beginning of the course and review your study materials. This should not be too difficult, because if you have been following my study methods all along, you should have been able to learn and remember the subject throughout the course.

Regardless of the scope of the final exam, you will be facing a very heavy study workload at the end of the semester or year. This is a very special period because many of your instructors will want to give their final exams. To get ready for these exams, you should take a very close look at your schedule a month (or at least a few weeks) ahead of time to see what will be expected of you. You can then work your way back from each of the final exams to determine when you need to begin studying for each one. If your schedule is very busy and you will need to take several final exams, you may need to start studying sooner than you would have started earlier in the term.

When studying for a final exam, you should use a slightly different approach than when studying for regular exams. Exams given throughout the semester or year usually test your understanding of very specific subjects. On the other hand, final exams usually test your understanding of large themes or ideas that your instructor presented throughout the course. As you study for a final exam, look for these large themes or ideas that seem to run through the various subjects you studied. This should not be too difficult if you have been following my study methods, because your earlier preparation helped you understand the various subjects and see how they fit together. Once you have identified the major themes and ideas, you can then supplement them with the specific details that are relevant.

To prepare for a final exam, you should review all of the tests that you took earlier during the semester or year. Although your teacher will probably not ask the same questions on the final exam, they may be of a similar type and pattern. Moreover, the answers to these earlier questions may be part of an answer to a broader question asked on the final exam.

Make sure that you understand the complete answer to all of the questions asked on earlier tests, particularly if you missed part or all of them. Most instructors review exams when they return them to students, and indicate what was expected for a good answer. You should have been taking careful notes during these reviews, just as you would during a regular lecture. If you do not know the complete answer to a question on an earlier exam, do not hesitate to see your instructor for clarification. Your goal should be to go into the final exam with complete knowledge of everything that was presented in the course, so you will not make the same mistakes again.

In preparing for a final exam, it is also helpful to review final exams from previous semesters or years to see what questions your instructor asked. Some instructors keep a file of past final exams, and make them available to students through the department, library, or online. If these are not available, you may be able to obtain a copy of the previous final exam from a fraternal organization, if you are in college. Or you might talk to students in a grade or year ahead of you who took the course to see if they saved the final exam, or possibly remember some of the questions that were asked.

Because it is unlikely that your instructor will ask the same questions again, when you look at previous final exams do not try to memorize or write complete answers to the questions. The main idea is to get a feel for the types of questions your instructor asks on final exams. For example, look at the number of questions asked, the types of subjects they covered, whether they were essay or objective questions, and the amount of time that students had to answer them. By the end of the semester or year, you should already have a good idea of your instructor's MO on regular exams, but he or she may decide to do something different on the final exam.

Your frame of mind during the period when final exams are given will be an important determinant of your performance. You should approach your final exams with a tranquil mind, to realize your highest level of achievement. If you have allowed yourself enough time to study, then you should be able to take your exams in a confident and relaxed manner. If, like most students, you have not allowed yourself enough time, the whole experience will be similar to a fraternal hell week and you will not do your best.

Be very conscious of how you use your time to study for final exams, because if you are not vigilant your time may quickly slip away. Work very hard and work consistently, but still allow enough time for breaks so you will not burn yourself out. Think about other leisure activities that you might cut back on during this period, and then reward yourself with them after all of your final exams are over.

You should not be concerned that the final exam is the biggest test of the entire course, and that it will play a significant part in your final grade. Take the final exam as you would take any other exam, and concentrate on doing your best, and everything else should fall into place!

RECAP

To earn top marks on your final exams:

1. Know what material will be covered on each final exam.
2. Start studying for all of your final exams well ahead of time.
3. Look for major themes or ideas that run throughout the courses.
4. Review previous final exams.
5. Show your teachers what you have learned.

Be relaxed and confident to perform at your highest level!

RECAP

A System for Getting Straight A's
(A proven ten-point study system that will put you on the road to success)

1. Plan a Course of Study (pages 186–194)
   (And always take the right subjects)

2. Choose Your Instructors if You Can (pages 194–201)
   (But always work with your instructors if you cannot)

3. Never Miss a Class (pages 201–206)
   (But always make up the work if it cannot be helped)

4. Always Sit in the Front Row (pages 207–210)
   (Or get as close to the front row as possible)

5. Always Complete Your Homework Assignments Before Class (pages 211–217)
   (So you will understand lectures and be prepared for questions)

6. Take Extensive Notes in Class (pages 218–227)
   (So you will become an active listener and retain more information)

7. Review (or Rewrite) Your Lecture Notes Before the Next Class (pages 227–236)
   (To get everything in order, and start studying for the next test)

8. Start Reviewing Your Lecture Notes and Reading Materials One Week Before a Test (pages 236–247)
   (So you will be fully prepared to take it)

9. **Be Testwise and Confident When Taking a Test (pages 247–255)**
(Because these are the qualities that lead to success)

10. **Show Your Instructor What You Have Learned on the Final Exam (pages 255–259)**
(Because it is a big part of your final grade)

8

Making the System Work for You

(Helpful study tips that will make your task easier and more enjoyable)

Rudyard Kipling, British author of many classics in children's literature, wrote in the poem "The Elephant's Child":

> *I keep six honest serving men*
> *(They taught me all I knew);*
> *Their names are What and Why and When*
> *And How and Where and Who.*

You will not need to ask two of the serving men *Who* will be studying (You!) and *Why* it is important to study (if you have been listening to your parents and read the first part of this book). But the other four serving men have important advice on the proper methods of study, so let's listen to what they have to say.

The main idea of this chapter is that it is not enough to know how to become a good student, you must actively practice the proper study habits to accomplish your goals. If you are to become a straight-A student, you must know *when, where, what, and how* to study, and how to practice good study habits and avoid bad ones. That is why I have titled this chapter "Making the System Work for You."

When to Study

If you want to become a better student, you need to be studying something every day. This does not mean that you should be studying continuously every day, or studying the same amount each day, but it does mean that you should be accomplishing something every day if you want to make progress in becoming a better student.

To organize your time, you should use calendars in a constructive manner. This does not mean that you should fill out detailed calendars laying out what you will be doing every second, minute, and hour for each day during the entire school term. Such regimentation would be very boring, and you probably would not be willing to follow it anyway. What I am in favor of is writing down *significant* dates on a calendar. For example, you should write down dates for tests, or when homework assignments or papers are due. By glancing at these dates periodically, you will be able to allow yourself enough time to get prepared for significant events.

Your immediate planning horizon for setting up a study schedule should encompass only a few days at a time. You should have a good idea of what will be required in each of your courses over the next few days. For example, you will need to review or rewrite the lecture notes you took in class, complete some reading or writing assignments, prepare for one or more tests (if some are coming up), and possibly do other assignments as well. The idea is to allocate your time a few days in advance so you can complete all of the work that is due in your various courses, and still have some time left over to pursue your own leisure activities. By planning only a few days in advance, you will have the flexibility to make changes in your schedule that will lead to the most efficient use of time.

The way to make the best use of your time is to study during periods when there are no competing activities that you want to participate in. For example, if you have a favorite extracurricular activity or sporting event coming up, think about whether you want to be studying before or after the event. If you know that you are going to be very active with some activity tomorrow, perhaps you should study an extra amount today to compensate.

You can also make efficient use of your time by studying before, between, or after classes. For example, you might be able to squeeze in some studying between the time when you wake up and attend your first class. You might be able to catch up on your reading assignments, or review or rewrite your lecture notes, between classes when you would normally be wasting your time. Rather than taking that extra-long lunch hour to shoot the bull with your friends, you might be able to accomplish something on your studies instead. The favorite time for goofing off seems to be when classes are over for the day, and this is often time that could have been used more productively for studying.

The way you spend your time for studying will depend mostly on the hours that you want to keep open for leisure. As I have noted, some students like to take their leisure time immediately after getting home from school, whereas others prefer to take it later in the evening. I recommend that you start studying as soon as you get home from school, so you can get your work done and not have to worry about it or run short of time later on. Always remember that you need to have some leisure time every day, or you could burn yourself out. The best approach is to use leisure as a reward for getting work done, and that is why I put work first.

Where to Study

Making a choice on where to study is more important than you might at first think, because it will influence how effectively you study. You should select a location where you feel very comfortable, can concentrate deeply, and are able to accomplish a significant amount of work. Some students find that they can study best in a certain chair or room in their house. They feel very comfortable in this spot, and think of it as a good place to study. Just make sure that you do not become too comfortable, such as lying down in bed, because you may doze off and accomplish less. Other students are more comfortable with studying in the library, because they like the atmosphere of being surrounded by books and seeing all of the other students at work. There is no single best spot for everyone, so you need to decide on the location that works best for *you*.

To use your time wisely, you should realize that there are many places to study other than your special place. For example, you could be thinking about the subjects you are studying when getting dressed in the morning, eating meals, waiting for or riding in a school bus, walking or driving to school, or any other time when your mind does not need to be engaged in a specific activity. When you are with your classmates, either in school or out of school, there will be opportunities to discuss the subjects you are studying. From my days in college, I remember numerous stimulating discussions that I had with my friends and professors after class was over for the day. This is similar to studying because you are forced to rethink and express ideas you have just learned. The discussions are particularly stimulating when an interdisciplinary group gets together to explore the various dimensions of a subject.

Regardless of the location where you decide to study, always remember that what is going on inside your head is more important than what is going on around you. Many students have difficulty concentrating and become fatigued after a few hours of studying. The problem is often more serious if they are in noisy surroundings or if the noise level changes back and forth from noisy to quiet. Sometimes students are more distracted by their internal frame of mind than by external phenomena. For example, if you are in the library and it is supposed to be quiet, you may be distracted by people talking, even if they are whispering. Or you may be distracted by a roommate who periodically taps his or her fingers on the desktop while studying. If you are really interested in a subject, however, you can usually focus on it and ignore distractions such as noise or other disturbances. The power of concentration is an important quality that will help you not only in school, but in everything else you do during your lifetime.

What to Study

By now you should have a good idea of the various things that you need to do to become a good student, but more is required. You know that you need to do your various reading and written assignments on schedule, review or rewrite your notes before the next class, and prepare for any upcoming tests. Now it is important for you to know what subjects to study, and in what order, as well as how much to study.

It is important to plan your activities every time you study. As soon as you sit down to do your studies each day, think about what you want to accomplish by the end of the study period. Think about the subject you will study first, and how much you will get done, then what subject you will study next, and how much you will get done, and so on for all of your subjects. Think about specific goals: how many pages you will read in your history book, the number of mathematics and science problems you will solve, or how many pages you will write for your English paper. Do your best to accomplish your goal every time you sit down to study. By working hard every day, and meeting your goals, you will experience a genuine sense of accomplishment.

It is always best to think about how much you will accomplish rather than how long you will study. If you worry about how long to study each subject, you may end watching the clock and accomplish less. As you formulate your goals, try to be realistic about what you can reasonably accomplish. Avoid setting goals that are so ambitious that you will never be able to accomplish them, because this could lead to frustration.

As you think about the order of subjects to study, try to add some variety that will make your work more interesting. For example, if you spend an extensive amount of time solving mathematics problems, you might follow this up by reading a chapter in your English or history book. Try to mix your studying on subjects you like with those you are not fond of. For example, if you are not crazy about science but love English, reward yourself by reading a novel after finishing your science assignment. By mixing the order of subjects in this manner, you may be able to study for a longer period of time without getting bored or tired.

You should spend a proportionate amount of time studying all of your subjects. Some students concentrate on the subjects they like and ignore the rest, but this is the wrong attitude. Never neglect a subject because you find it boring or difficult. These are the subjects that you should expend the most effort on. You goal should be to make A's in all of your courses, not just the ones you like. A spotty academic record raises questions about a student's ability or discipline. If you neglect a boring course for too long, you may fall so far behind that you are never able to catch up. This will make matters worse later on, and you may end up getting a poor grade in the course. Always strive to be a well-rounded person in everything you do!

How to Study

When you sit down to study, you should have a serious attitude and be willing to study very hard. If there is something else that you need to get done before studying, then get it out of the way first so it will not be a distraction. Never put off studying because you dislike a subject, or because you feel tired or lazy. Face the fact that you are going to have to do the work sooner or later, so you might as well get it out of the way sooner. What is required is self-discipline, which means that you will do what you have to do when you are supposed to do it, whether you like it or not!

When you actually start to study, you should throw yourself into your work, and not let anything else interfere or cause a distraction. This means that you will need the energy, enthusiasm, and determination to get your work done every time you study. If you are having a hard time getting into your studies, it sometimes helps if you start off with something easy and work your way up to the more difficult subject matter. Students often put off doing work because they keep thinking how difficult it will be. When they finally get started, the work is easier than they expected, and they regret procrastinating for so long.

Students who get the most done have the power of concentration. When you are studying, concentrate only on the subject at hand, and block everything else out of your mind. Avoid thinking about other subjects, what you will do after studying, your social life, what sports you enjoy, or anything else that is irrelevant. Never try to do two or more things at the same time, because you will end up doing none of them very well. When you are studying, do not also try to watch television, play video games, or carry on a conversation with your friends on the telephone. Concentrate on the business at hand—studying!

You will be able to accomplish much more if you study for long periods of time rather than short ones. When you study continuously, you do not have to keep going back to review where you left off the last time you studied. You will also be able to relate ideas in different segments of your studies more effectively because they will still be fresh in your mind. Weekends are a particularly good time to study, because you have long blocks of time without any interruptions. Get up early on the weekend, and you will be surprised at how much you can get done before anyone else awakens. Never study for so long, however, that you begin to feel tired or worn out, because this will be counterproductive.

When you are studying for long periods of time, always be sure to allow time for breaks. Take breaks whenever you need a breather from one subject, or you are shifting over to another one. It is a good idea to take a five- or ten-minute break every hour to recharge your batteries. Never take an excessive number of breaks, however, or make them too long, because this will get in the way of your studying. There are any number of things you can do during your breaks, such as chatting with friends, watching television or listening to radio, doing chores around the house, or just doing nothing to relax. The important thing is to do whatever *you* want, so you can return to your studies feeling refreshed and ready to go back to work.

If you have been studying for most of the day, it is important to leave time in the evening for winding down. Do not study all of the way up to the time when you are ready to go to bed, because you will probably be too wound up to fall asleep. Take some time to do something fun, such as talking to friends, reading a good novel, watching a favorite television program, or surfing the Internet. You might even spend some time getting things ready for school the next day, so you will not have to hurry the following morning. If you lie down in bed after studying so hard, you will probably be wide awake with your head spinning like a top.

Practice Good Habits

An important aspect of having good study habits is to have good habits in general. You will be a much better student if you are healthy. Always get plenty of rest, because it is difficult to concentrate if you are tired or have a headache. It is also important to eat properly, something students are not known to do. Eat three balanced meals a day—including breakfast!—and avoid eating an excessive amount of junk food. I know it is sometimes difficult to get a nutritious meal from the food served in school cafeterias, but do the best you can. You will not be able to work hard at your studies if you do not have any energy.

You will also be a better student if you are physically fit. Students spend a lot of time sitting in class and studying after school, so it is important to get up and move around afterward. Regardless of age, everyone needs to have a regular exercise program. I like distance walking, lifting light weights, and playing tennis, but there is any number of other ways to get exercise, such as jogging, swimming, or practicing some form of aerobics program. Depending on your level in school, physical education programs are often available. Alternatively, you might join a gym or perform a regular exercise program at home. In addition, you might want to add to your exercise program by joining a team in your favorite sport. Like a trained athlete, you will perform better mentally when you are fit physically.

Avoid Bad Habits

I know you have heard the advice I am about to give a thousand times or more, but it does not hurt to hear it again. Avoid taking harmful substances into your body, such as tobacco, alcohol, and drugs. Not only will they destroy your health, you will not perform your best as a student. Moreover, you may get into much more serious trouble that will disrupt your education plans altogether.

Sometimes activities that are normally acceptable become bad habits when we do them for too long. For example, there is nothing wrong with watching your favorite television program every day. However, if you spend several hours a day watching television, this is excessive, and will leave a lot less time for studying. Surfing the Internet, playing video games, listening to music, and conversing with your friends are examples of other activities that could become obsessive and eat up your time. It is okay to do these things in moderation, as long as they do not get out of hand and interfere with your studies. If you are having difficulty controlling how much time you spend on these activities, it may be wise to follow the advice of the American humorist Mark Twain, often given to compulsive gamblers: "It is easier to stay out than get out."

Practice Time Management

It is a fact of life that most people, both adults and children alike, are not very efficient in how they use their time, whether they are in school or doing something else. To become more efficient as a student, you could practice something called "time management," which is an approach to using time better.

To apply time management to your life as a student, take a close look at how you spend an average school day. Make some notes on the time that you got up, how long it took you to get ready for school, what you did at school, especially during breaks, and what you did when you got home from school that day. When you got home, did you start studying right away, or goof off for a while? When you finally did start studying, did you make the best use of your time, or allow other things to get in your way? Now think about how you might have done some things differently. I think you will find that you could have arranged your schedule differently to free up a lot more time for studying, and still have had plenty of time left over for leisure activities!

If you have not been using your time wisely, you probably need to make some changes in your schedule. It is very difficult to make big changes all at once, so you could start with some small changes. Look for some small blocks of time that could easily have been used for studying without disrupting other activities. After a while, you can add some more small changes, which together will add up to big changes, and before you know it you will have a better way of getting things done. Once you have your schedule in order, you will find that you can get more things done in a shorter period of time.

As you think about how to use your time more wisely, I want to warn you not to go overboard and devote all of your time to studying. You can overdo studying, just as you can overdo anything else in life. If you spend all of your time studying, you will not have time for other activities and your life will become quite boring indeed. Your goal should be to study enough to make A's in all of your courses and still have time left over to do all of the other things that you want to do. You can do it all if you have a good system of study and you apply your time wisely, and the purpose of this book is to show you the way!

As you grow older and gain more experience, you will find that the people who are the best at what they do—whatever it is—are the ones who have a special way of approaching life. Successful people are goal oriented, focused, and hard working. This is true regardless of their occupation, whether they are a doctor, lawyer, publisher, salesperson, craftsman, sanitary engineer, or just about any other occupation you can think of. The same is true of students. If you develop the right study habits now, you will find that it is easier to become a better student and you will be better at your job when you get out of school. Simply put, you will be *making the system work for you*!

RECAP

Studying will be much easier and more rewarding if you:

1. Know *when, where, what,* and *how* to study
2. Practice good habits and avoid bad ones
3. Practice time management

It's a Wrap

"From the end spring new beginnings," said Pliny the Elder, the ancient Roman philosopher who was also known for his brilliance as a military commander. I have come to my end, but the whole purpose of the journey was to spring a new beginning for *you*!

In this book I have told you everything I know about how to become a straight-A student. I have reviewed the successes of several other students who have risen to the top and discussed the importance of a high-quality education. You have learned several important skills that will enable you to perform at the highest level in school. I have shown you how to read books and get the most from them, how to take several different types of tests, and how to write papers that are informative and interesting to read. I have presented an entire study system that shows you how to take the right subjects, get the most from your classes, prepare homework assignments, study for tests, and make the highest marks on tests.

Finally, I have shown you how to develop good study habits so you can get all of your work done in an efficient manner, and still have plenty of time left over for other activities.

With all of this knowledge, can you now expect to become a straight-A student? The answer is no, it is not that easy—much more is required! It is not enough to know something, you have to practice it diligently to achieve the benefits.

If you want to become a top student, then you need to follow *all* of the steps in my study system *all* of the time. You will need to follow each of these steps not just occasionally, but throughout the entire semester or year. If you do anything less than this, you will not really be following my study system, and you will not get the best results. I have learned this lesson through the many students I have worked with over the years, and through my own personal experiences. Few have the discipline and willpower to follow my study system completely, but those who do get impressive results. If you follow all of the steps all of the time you will see the greatest improvement, and if you follow some of the steps some of the time you may see little or no improvement.

Even though you have learned the best way to study and prepare for tests, you will need to work very hard to reach the top. I cannot wave a magic wand to relieve you of the workload. Hard work is the only true road to success. American inventor Thomas Edison, who was one of the greatest geniuses of all time, probably said it best: "Genius is one percent inspiration and ninety-nine percent perspiration." In other words, it is not enough to be smart—you have to work very hard to succeed! Edison was known for his wonderful inventions such as the phonograph and a long-lasting lightbulb, but most people think only of his successes and not all of the hard work and failure he experienced before making a breakthrough.

To work very hard, you will need to be highly motivated. What does it take for you to get highly motivated? You will need to be interested in what you are doing, feel that it is very important, and have the ambition to work very hard to accomplish your goals. Specifically, you must have the energy and drive to follow through with your actions. When you are truly motivated, you will always do your best, are unwilling to settle for anything less than your best, and keep trying no matter how difficult the situation!

The main reason that students have difficulty in getting motivated for school is that they think they would rather be doing something else. They often think, "If only I could get out of school, I would not have to do any more boring homework, and I could get a job and make some money." Then, when they finally do get out into the working world later on, they find that it is far more of a grind than school, and often more boring. You should think of the situation in the following way: You are part of a captive audience. You are going to be in school for a certain amount of time anyway, so you might as well work very hard and put forth your best effort!

Think of the rewards of being a good student and penalties for being a poor one. If you make good grades in school, this will help you get into a good college, and if you are already in college, good grades will help you get a good job later on. If you do not have a good education, and your grades are very poor, you may end up in a boring job in which you will still have to work very hard but will not make much money. *The consequences are huge!*

It is important for you to put forth your best effort as a student at an *early* age, while there is still enough time to get into a good occupation that will bring large financial returns later on. Some employers are less willing to hire older workers because they think that they are less adaptable. Many people work harder and become more productive as they mature, but their efforts sometimes come a little too late. If you get into a good occupation at an early age, you have a whole lifetime to advance up the job ladder and get a good return on the investment you made in education. Without the proper education, or if it comes too late, you may end up in a low-skilled, boring occupation that will break your back, your spirit, and your pocketbook!

If you are still having difficulty getting motivated, then I have a final exercise for you. Take out a sheet of paper and write down your goals in life. List very specific things such as the type of job you want to enter, where you want to live, how much money you want to make, and what you want to do when you retire. Then think about what you will need to do to accomplish these goals. I will bet that a good education plays a significant role in your plans. Put this sheet away in a place where you can easily find it, and look at it from time to time when you are not feeling motivated. Then remind yourself that all of the hard work is for *you*!

It is important for you to recognize that it is impossible to accomplish all of your goals immediately. Even if you are working very hard and following everything that I have laid out in this book, it may take you a while to become a straight-A student. The more we work at anything in life, the better we become at doing it, and school is no exception. It takes time to develop good study habits and all of the skills that are needed to perform at the highest level in school. As you follow my study methods, you should start to see some improvements in your grades right away, and that by itself should give you some satisfaction. The proper attitude is to concentrate on what you need to do to become a straight-A student, rather than expecting to become one immediately!

It is also important for you to realize that sometimes you will need to push yourself to the limit in school. Even though I received an A on every test in every course I took in graduate school, there were times when the going got quite rough.

Sometimes things get so rough that you feel like you are in the middle of a war. Everything may seem to be happening at once—term papers are due and tests are given back-to-back, all in a matter of a few days. At these times, you need to keep a strong frame of mind, rise to the occasion, and fight back to prevail. Here is some advice from someone who knows a lot about war, "Old Blood and Guts" himself, General George S. Patton: "The most vital quality a soldier can possess is self-confidence, utter, complete and bumptious." That is the same kind of self-confidence you will need when you feel that you are in a war with your studies!

You should also realize that even if you have worked your hardest in school, done everything that is necessary, and have utter self-confidence, it is impossible to be perfect. We are all human beings, and we are going to make some mistakes and have some disappointments. I have had plenty of my own. The proper attitude is to not let these upset you. If you have been following my study system, you should start to see some progress right away, and you will do even better in the future because you are on the right track. You will also get more enjoyment out of your schoolwork, because we all enjoy the things that we do well. A certain feeling of pride comes from being a good student, so this is something that you can look forward to.

What can you expect to get for all of your efforts in school? I described several of them in an earlier chapter, "The Value of Getting Good Grades," but some of them are worth repeating here. Researchers have found that students who do well in school are more likely to have success in other parts of their lives. Good students are more likely to have friends, participate in extracurricular activities, and hold school offices. They are also more likely to be successful when they get out of school and enter the working world, in terms of getting better jobs and having a more comfortable standard of living.

More broadly, a good education influences just about every aspect of your life. A real sense of satisfaction comes from obtaining knowledge and understanding how the world works, as I pointed out in the first part of this book. In summary, a good education makes you a more complete person!

We have come to the end of a long journey, and I hope it was as enjoyable for you to read as it was for me to write. The main reason that I write study guides such as this one is that I enjoy helping other people. You now know what your mission is—to become a straight-A student!—and how to accomplish it. Many people have told me that they wish they had known the things in this book when they were younger, because school would have been more enjoyable and rewarding. I hope that you are reading this book at a young enough age so you do not have to make the same statement. I wish you great success in your studies, and invite you to tell me about your accomplishments. You can reach me through my publisher, whose address is listed at the front of the book.

I will leave you with one final thought that is the most important thing I have said in this book. It is one of the first things you read in this book, and I want it also to be the last thing you read so you will remember it when you put the book down. It is a surefire formula for success that will never let you down: *Never give up!*

RECAP

Parents and students:
The secret of success is constancy to purpose.

—*Benjamin Disraeli,*
former British prime minister

Appendix A

Recommended Reading List

The following is a recommended reading list of 101 great books for college-bound students from the College Board, a not-for-profit organization whose mission is to promote college success and opportunity. The best-known programs at the College Board are the SAT, PSAT/NMSQT, and Advanced Placement (AP) Program.

Author	Title
——	*Beowulf*
Achebe, Chinua	*Things Fall Apart*
Agee, James	*A Death in the Family*
Austen, Jane	*Pride and Prejudice*
Baldwin, James	*Go Tell It on the Mountain*
Beckett, Samuel	*Waiting for Godot*
Bellow, Saul	*The Adventures of Augie March*

Source: *101 Great Books.* Copyright © 2009, the College Board. www.college board.com. Reprinted with permission.

Author	Title
Brontë, Charlotte	*Jane Eyre*
Brontë, Emily	*Wuthering Heights*
Camus, Albert	*The Stranger*
Cather, Willa	*Death Comes for the Archbishop*
Chaucer, Geoffrey	*The Canterbury Tales*
Chekhov, Anton	*The Cherry Orchard*
Chopin, Kate	*The Awakening*
Conrad, Joseph	*Heart of Darkness*
Cooper, James Fenimore	*The Last of the Mohicans*
Crane, Stephen	*The Red Badge of Courage*
Dante	*Inferno*
de Cervantes, Miguel	*Don Quixote*
Defoe, Daniel	*Robinson Crusoe*
Dickens, Charles	*A Tale of Two Cities*
Dostoyevsky, Fyodor	*Crime and Punishment*
Douglass, Frederick	*Narrative of the Life of Frederick Douglass*
Dreiser, Theodore	*An American Tragedy*
Dumas, Alexandre	*The Three Musketeers*
Eliot, George	*The Mill on the Floss*
Ellison, Ralph	*Invisible Man*
Emerson, Ralph Waldo	*Selected Essays*
Faulkner, William	*As I Lay Dying*
Faulkner, William	*The Sound and the Fury*
Fielding, Henry	*Tom Jones*
Fitzgerald, F. Scott	*The Great Gatsby*
Flaubert, Gustave	*Madame Bovary*
Ford, Ford Madox	*The Good Soldier*
Goethe, Johann Wolfgang von	*Faust*
Golding, William	*Lord of the Flies*
Hardy, Thomas	*Tess of the d'Urbervilles*
Hawthorne, Nathaniel	*The Scarlet Letter*
Heller, Joseph	*Catch 22*

Author	Title
Hemingway, Ernest	*A Farewell to Arms*
Homer	*The Iliad*
Homer	*The Odyssey*
Hugo, Victor	*The Hunchback of Notre Dame*
Hurston, Zora Neale	*Their Eyes Were Watching God*
Huxley, Aldous	*Brave New World*
Ibsen, Henrik	*A Doll's House*
James, Henry	*The Portrait of a Lady*
James, Henry	*The Turn of the Screw*
Joyce, James	*A Portrait of the Artist as a Young Man*
Kafka, Franz	*The Metamorphosis*
Kingston, Maxine Hong	*The Woman Warrior*
Lee, Harper	*To Kill a Mockingbird*
Lewis, Sinclair	*Babbitt*
London, Jack	*The Call of the Wild*
Mann, Thomas	*The Magic Mountain*
Marquez, Gabriel García	*One Hundred Years of Solitude*
Melville, Herman	*Bartleby the Scrivener*
Melville, Herman	*Moby Dick*
Miller, Arthur	*The Crucible*
Morrison, Toni	*Beloved*
O'Connor, Flannery	*A Good Man Is Hard to Find*
O'Neill, Eugene	*Long Day's Journey into Night*
Orwell, George	*Animal Farm*
Pasternak, Boris	*Doctor Zhivago*
Plath, Sylvia	*The Bell Jar*
Poe, Edgar Allan	*Selected Tales*
Proust, Marcel	*Swann's Way*
Pynchon, Thomas	*The Crying of Lot 49*
Remarque, Erich Maria	*All Quiet on the Western Front*
Rostand, Edmond	*Cyrano de Bergerac*
Roth, Henry	*Call It Sleep*
Salinger, J. D.	*The Catcher in the Rye*

Author	Title
Shakespeare, William	*Hamlet*
Shakespeare, William	*Macbeth*
Shakespeare, William	*A Midsummer Night's Dream*
Shakespeare, William	*Romeo and Juliet*
Shaw, George Bernard	*Pygmalion*
Shelley, Mary	*Frankenstein*
Silko, Leslie Marmon	*Ceremony*
Solzhenitsyn, Alexander	*One Day in the Life of Ivan Denisovich*
Sophocles	*Antigone*
Sophocles	*Oedipus Rex*
Steinbeck, John	*The Grapes of Wrath*
Stevenson, Robert Louis	*Treasure Island*
Stowe, Harriet Beecher	*Uncle Tom's Cabin*
Swift, Jonathan	*Gulliver's Travels*
Thackeray, William	*Vanity Fair*
Thoreau, Henry David	*Walden*
Tolstoy, Leo	*War and Peace*
Turgenev, Ivan	*Fathers and Sons*
Twain, Mark	*The Adventures of Huckleberry Finn*
Voltaire	*Candide*
Vonnegut, Kurt, Jr.	*Slaughterhouse Five*
Walker, Alice	*The Color Purple*
Wharton, Edith	*The House of Mirth*
Welty, Eudora	*Collected Stories*
Whitman, Walt	*Leaves of Grass*
Wilde, Oscar	*The Picture of Dorian Gray*
Williams, Tennessee	*The Glass Menagerie*
Woolf, Virginia	*To the Lighthouse*
Wright, Richard	*Native Son*

Appendix B

Key Words Used in Examinations*

Key Items of Quantity, Duration, or Degree

All, always	Necessarily	—any exception
Only	Necessary	makes these
Without exception	Never	statements false
	No, none	

Rarely	Almost always	—imply a judgment
Seldom, Infrequent(ly)	Usual(ly), Often,	of frequency or
Occasional(ly)	Frequent(ly)	probability
Some, Sometimes	Probably	
Few	Many	
Several	Most	
About, Around	Approximate(ly)	

*As printed in Gordon W. Green Jr., Ph.D., *Getting Straight A's,* Carol Publishing Group, New York, 1993.

Descriptive and Analysis Questions

Describe, Review
— give account of the attributes of the subject under discussion (inherent characteristics, qualities)

Discuss
— tell all you know about the subject that is relevant to the questions under consideration

State
— briefly "describe" with minimal elaboration

Analyze
— separate the subject into parts and examine the elements of which it is composed

Enumerate, List, Tabulate
— briefly present the sequence of elements constituting the whole

Develop
— from a given starting point, evolve a logical pattern leading to a valid conclusion

Trace
— in narrative form, describe the progress, development, or historical events related to a specific topic from some point of time to a stated conclusion

Outline, Summarize
— give the theme and main points of the subject in concise form

Diagram, Sketch
— outline the principal *distinguishing* features of an object or process using a clearly labeled diagram

Explanation and Proof Questions

Explain, Interpret
— state the subject in simpler, more explicit terms

Define, Formulate
— classify the subject; specify its unique qualities and characteristics

Prove,   — demonstrate validity by test, argument,
  Justify,   or evidence
  Show that

Demonstrate   — explain or prove by use of significant examples

Illustrate   — explain fully by means of diagrams, charts,
                   or concrete examples

Comparison Questions

Compare   — investigate and state the likeness or
                  similarities of two or more subjects

Contrast   — look for noticeable differences

Relate   — establish the connection between one or
                  more things

Personal Judgment Questions

Criticize,   — judge or evaluate the subject for its truth,
  Evaluate   beauty, worth, or significance; and justify
                  your evaluation. "Criticize" does not
                  necessarily mean a hostile attack—it is
                  more a matter of comment on literal or
                  implied meaning.

Interpret   — explain and evaluate in terms of your own
                  knowledge

Justify   — ordinarily this implies that you justify a
                  statement on the author's terms. When
                  asked to justify your own statements, defend
                  your position in detail and be convincing.

Problem/Solution Questions

Find,   — using the data provided (some of which may be
  Solve,   irrelevant) apply mathematical procedures and
  Calculate,   the principles of formal logical analysis to find
  Determine,   a specific quantity in specific units
  Derive,
  What is . . . ?

Appendix C

Educational Resources

Student Loans and Financial Aid

U.S. Department of Education, Federal Student Aid, Direct Loan Program, http://www.ed.gov/offices/OSFAP/DirectLoan/index.html.

U.S. Department of Education, Federal Student Aid, Financial Aid, http://www.ed.gov/finaid/landing.jhtml?src=ln.

FinAid! The SmartStudent Guide to Financial Aid, http://www.finaid.org/.

Statistics on Income, Education, and Occupation

U.S. Census Bureau, Income, http://www.census.gov/hhes/www/income/income.html.

U.S. Census Bureau, Educational Attainment, http://pubdb3.census.gov/macro/032008/perinc/new03_000.htm.

U.S. Census Bureau, Occupation of Longest Job, http://pubdb3.census.gov/macro/032008/perinc/new06_000.htm.

U.S. Bureau of Labor Statistics, Occupational Outlook Handbook, http://www.bls.gov/OCO/.

Obtaining Credit Before Entering College

College Board, Advanced Placement (AP), http://www.collegeboard
.com/student/testing/ap/about.html.

College Board, College-Level Examination Program (CLEP), http://
www.collegeboard.com/student/testing/clep/about.html.

International Baccalaureate Organization, International Baccalaureate (IB) Diploma Programme (DP), http://www.ibo.org/.

University of Cambridge, Cambridge International Examinations
(CIE), http://www.cie.org.uk/.

Entrance Examinations for College and Graduate School

College Board, SAT, http://www.collegeboard.com/student/testing/
sat/about.html.

College Board, Preliminary SAT (PSAT)/ National Merit Scholarship Qualifying Test (NMSQT), http://www.collegeboard.com/
student/testing/psat/about.html.

Educational Testing Service, Graduate Record Examination (GRE),
http://www.ets.org/gre/.

Organizations that Promote and Coordinate Foreign Study

American Field Service, http://www.afs.org/afs_or/home.

American Institute for Foreign Study, http://www.aifs.com/.

Council for Standards on International Education Travel, http://
www.csiet.org/mc/page.do.

Rotary Youth Exchange, http://www.rotary.org/en/StudentsAnd
Youth/youthprograms/RotaryYouthExchange/Pages/ridefault
.aspx.

Youth for Understanding Foundation, http://yfu.org.

Appendix D

Dr. Green's Academic Transcript
for a Ph.D. in Economics

TRANSCRIPT GUIDE PRINTED ON REVERSE

THE GEORGE WASHINGTON UNIVERSITY
WASHINGTON, D.C. 20006
OFFICE OF THE REGISTRAR

Degree Awarded: Ph.D. 20–FEB–1984
Major: Economics

PERMANENT RECORD

LAST NAME	FIRST	MIDDLE
GREEN	GORDON	WOODROW

SEX	DATE OF BIRTH	PLACE OF BIRTH
M/F	1/14/47	WASHINGTON, D.C.

ADVANCED STANDING: B.S. 1968, UNIVERSITY OF MARYLAND;
DIVISION ADMITTED: GRAD SCH ARTS & SCI.(DOCT)
DATE ADMITTED: SPRING 1976

SEE DEGREE ENTRY IN BODY OF RECORD

DEPT.	COURSE NO.	COURSE TITLE		SEM. HR.	GRADE	QUAL. POINTS
		SPRING 1976	408877			
ECON	205	MACROECON THEORY		3	A	12
ECON	208	NATIONAL INCOME		3	A	12
		FALL 1976	408877			
ECON	203	MICROECON THEORY		3	A	12
ECON	215	MATHEMATICAL ECON		3	A	12
		SPRING 1977	408877			
ECON	204	MICROECON THEORY		3	A	12
ECON	216	MATHEMATICAL ECON		3	A	12
		FALL 1977	408877			
ECON	206	MACROECON THEORY 2		3	A	12
ECON	275	ECONOMETRICS 1		3	A	12
		SPRING 1978	408877			
ECON	202	HIST OF ECON THOT		3	A	12
ECON	276	ECONOMETRICS 2		3	A	12
		FALL 1978	408877			
ECON	263	THRY PUB FINANCE 1		3	A	12
OR	201	(SPRTNS RSCH MTHD 1)		3	A	12
		SPRING 1979	408877			
ECON	264	THRY PUB FINANCE 2		3	A	12
OR	202	OPRTNS RSCH MTHD 2		3	A	12
		FALL 1979	408877			
ECON	241	LABOR ECONOMICS		3	A	12
ECON	379	READ IN ECON HIST		3	A	12
		SPRING 1980	408877			
ECON	242	LABOR ECONOMICS		3	A	12
ECON	259	INCOME DISTRIBUTN		3	A	12
		FALL 1980	408877			
ECON	398	ADV READING&RESRCH		3	A	12

DEGREE CONFERRED: M.PHIL. 2/16/81
MAJOR: ECONOMICS

PASSED PH.D. GENERAL EXAMINATION IN ECONOMICS 5/27/80
PASSED PH.D. GENERAL EXAMINATION IN PUBLIC FINANCE 9-7-79
PASSED TOOL EXAMINATION SPRING 1979
PASSED PH.D. GENERAL EXAMINATION IN MICROECONOMICS 9/8/77
PASSED PH.D. GENERAL EXAMINATION IN MACROECONOMICS 9/13/76
MATHEMATICAL STATISTICS REQUIREMENT WAIVED 3/5/76
FACULTY ACTION

This is a true copy of the official record of the above named student. When signed and sealed with the impression seal of this office it constitutes an official transcript or record. Honorable dismissal granted unless otherwise stated under faculty section.

UNIVERSITY REGISTRAR

THE WORD VOID APPEARS WHEN PHOTOCOPIED

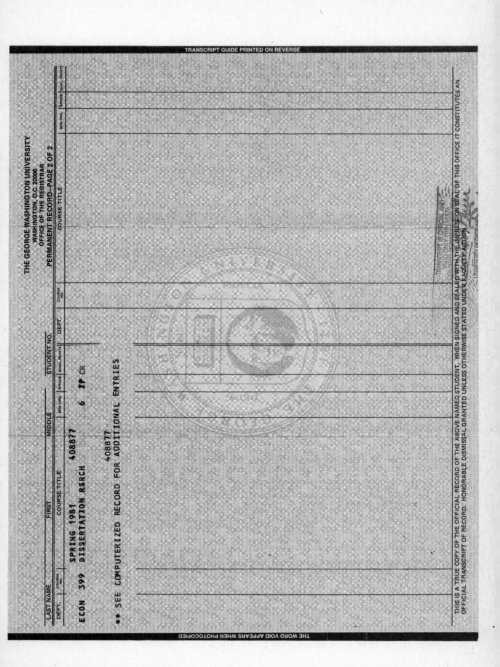

THE GEORGE WASHINGTON UNIVERSITY
WASHINGTON, D.C. 20006
OFFICE OF THE REGISTRAR
PERMANENT RECORD—PAGE 2 OF 2

LAST NAME	FIRST	MIDDLE	STUDENT NO.

DEPT.	COURSE NO.	COURSE TITLE	SEM. HRS.	GRADE	QUAL. POINTS
		SPRING 1981 408877			
ECON	399	DISSERTATION RSRCH	6	IP	CR
		408877			
**	SEE COMPUTERIZED RECORD FOR ADDITIONAL ENTRIES				

DEPT.	COURSE NO.	COURSE TITLE	SEM. HRS.	GRADE	QUAL. POINTS

The
George
Washington
University
WASHINGTON DC
OFFICE OF THE REGISTRAR

Student No: ▮▮▮▮▮▮▮
Date of Birth: 14-JAN-1947

Record of: Gordon Woodrow Green

Student Level: Graduate   Issued To: Gordon Green
Admit Term: Fall 1981

Current College(s):Graduate School of Arts & Sci
Current Major(s): Economics

Degree Awarded: PhD 20-FEB-1984
Major :Economics

SEE PRIOR RECORD UNDER STUDENT NUMBER 408877

Date Issued: 11-JAN-2002
Page: 1

```
SUBJ NO  COURSE TITLE              CRDT  GRD PTS
-------------------------------------------------

GEORGE WASHINGTON UNIVERSITY CREDIT:

Fall 1981
   Graduate School of Arts & Sci
   Economics
ECON 399 Dissertation Research     6.00 CR   0.00
    Ehrs  6.00 GPA-Hrs  0.00 Pts   0.00 GPA  0.00
    CUM   6.00 GPA-Hrs  0.00 Pts   0.00 GPA  0.00

Spring 1982

ECON 399 Dissertation Research     6.00 CR   0.00
    Ehrs  6.00 GPA-Hrs  0.00 Pts   0.00 GPA  0.00
    CUM  12.00 GPA-Hrs  0.00 Pts   0.00 GPA  0.00

Fall 1982

ECON 399 Dissertation Research     3.00 CR   0.00
    Ehrs  3.00 GPA-Hrs  0.00 Pts   0.00 GPA  0.00
    CUM  15.00 GPA-Hrs  0.00 Pts   0.00 GPA  0.00

Spring 1983

UNIV 982 Continuous Enrollment     0.00      0.00
    Ehrs  0.00 GPA-Hrs  0.00 Pts   0.00 GPA  0.00
    CUM  15.00 GPA-Hrs  0.00 Pts   0.00 GPA  0.00

Fall 1983

UNIV 982 Continuous Enrollment     0.00      0.00
    Ehrs  0.00 GPA-Hrs  0.00 Pts   0.00 GPA  0.00
    CUM  15.00 GPA-Hrs  0.00 Pts   0.00 GPA  0.00

**************** TRANSCRIPT TOTALS *****************
            Earned Hrs GPA Hrs Points   GPA

TOTAL INSTITUTION 15.00     0.00   0.00  0.00

OVERALL           15.00     0.00   0.00  0.00

################# END OF DOCUMENT #################
```

Index

About the Author

Dr. Gordon W. Green, Jr., is well qualified to write this book. He received an A in every graduate course he took en route to receiving a Ph.D. in economics from George Washington University in 1984. His Ph.D. dissertation received national attention, including a front-page article in *The New York Times,* articles in several other newspapers and magazines, and an appearance on national television to discuss his findings. This accomplishment was quite remarkable, considering that Dr. Green was attending graduate school part-time in the evening, working more than full-time at his regular job, and taking care of home and family responsibilities at the same time. Even with this busy schedule, he had plenty of time for leisure activities. Dr. Green attributes his success to a unique system of study that he developed, which is the subject of this book.

As an author, Dr. Green has written a number of books that help students succeed in school and workers succeed in their jobs. His first book, *Getting Straight A's* (1985), has been translated into Spanish, Polish, and Vietnamese, is used in colleges and universities around the world, and was advertised for many years in *Parade* magazine. Dr. Green has also helped people improve their performance at work, in his book titled *Getting Ahead at Work* (1989). His other earlier books on education include *Helping Your Child to Learn* (1994) and *Helping Your Child to Learn Math* (1995). Dr. Green directed his efforts to help younger students succeed in school in a book titled *How to Get Straight A's in School and Have Fun at the Same Time* (1999). In his latest effort, *Making Your*

Education Work for You (2010), Dr. Green brings together all his knowledge and experience to help students in high school, college, and graduate school work together with parents for success, engage in effective job planning, and receive the highest grades in school. This effort caps not only a lifetime of writing and scholarly research, but also a lifetime of working directly with students and workers in seminars to make the ideas and theories become a reality.

Dr. Green also has extensive experience in the world of work. At the U.S. Census Bureau, he directed the preparation of the nation's official statistics on income and poverty for many years, as well as statistics on labor force and wealth. He was also chief of the Governments Division at the U.S. Census Bureau, and a member of the president's Senior Executive Service, where he directed the preparation of statistics on government finances and employment, as well as education and criminal justice statistics. For the National Center for Education Statistics, which is part of the U.S. Department of Education, Dr. Green served as both the chair and vice-chair of the National Forum on Education Statistics, a forum comprised of leading education officials from all the states in the nation. At Independent Sector, he was vice president of research, and directed the preparation of a variety of statistics on the nonprofit sector. At the American Enterprise Institute for Public Policy Research and the University of Maryland Foundation, Inc., he served as the assistant director of the Welfare Reform Academy, concentrating on improving the measurement of poverty and income inequality. Dr. Green also does consulting work for Sentier Research, LLC., a company that provides demographic and economic statistics and analysis for businesses, governments, and international organizations. His work is widely published in government periodicals, magazines, and professional journals.

Dr. Green lives with his wife, Maureen, in Fairfax Station and Charlottesville, Virginia.